Tee Time Tales

or

Memoirs of a Scoring Marshal 1999–2019

by
Doug Fowler

Paul –

I hope you enjoy my wee book.
Best wishes,
Doug
25th December 2023

Published by New Generation Publishing in 2023

Copyright © Doug Fowler 2023

First Edition

The author asserts the moral right under the Copyright, Designs and Patents Act 1988 to be identified as the author of this work.

All Rights reserved. No part of this publication may be reproduced, stored in a retrieval system or transmitted, in any form or by any means without the prior consent of the author, nor be otherwise circulated in any form of binding or cover other than that which it is published and without a similar condition being imposed on the subsequent purchaser.

ISBN: 978-1-80369-746-8

www.newgeneration-publishing.com

New Generation Publishing

This book is dedicated to the memory of Andy Murdoch, Pete Clews, Julian Steed, David Low, John Hendzel, Dennis Miller, Bernard Brace, Mike Upham, Dave Cliffe, Steve Stoodley, Carey Hoon and Ronnie Hope - all of whom are sadly no longer around to play this wonderful game.

In addition, I would like to mention my daughter, Aly - and my son, Chris - who have listened patiently as I have recounted these stories over and over again!

Contents

Introduction (1999) v

CHAPTER 1 – The English Open (1999) The Journey Begins: . 1

CHAPTER 2 (2000) The English Open 17

CHAPTER 3 (2001) The Wales Open 30

CHAPTER 4 (2002) The Great North Open, The English Open & The Ryder Cup (The Belfry): 34

CHAPTER 5 (2003) The Wales Open & The Open (Royal St George's) 73

CHAPTER 6 (2004) The Wales Open & The British Masters .. 93

CHAPTER 7 (2005) The Wales Open & The Open (St Andrews) 98

CHAPTER 8 (2006) The Wales Open, The Open (Hoylake) & The Ryder Cup (K Club) 117

CHAPTER 9 (2007) The Wales Open 155

CHAPTER 10 (2008) The Wales Open & The British Masters 160

CHAPTER 11 (2010) The Open (St Andrews) 164

CHAPTER 12 (2011) The Open (Royal St George's) 176

CHAPTER 13 (2016) The Open (Troon) 186

CHAPTER 14 (2018) The Open (Carnoustie) 199

CHAPTER 15 (2019) The Open (Royal Portrush) 210

CHAPTER 16 (2022) The Future – The Open 2025 (Royal Portrush) 222

Acknowledgements 229

Appendix – Winners (The Open In Blue) And Runners Up In Brackets: 230

INTRODUCTION (1999)

This is the tale of how a high handicap golfer became involved in his beloved game of golf at its highest level when volunteering as a Marshal and Walking Scorer at some of the most prestigious tournaments in the world, i.e., the Ryder Cup Matches and The Open Championship, amongst other European Tour events in the United Kingdom.

I had seen marshals on golf courses whilst watching The Open Championship on television, and I believed that their only job was to keep the crowds quiet by holding up funny little boards marked 'Quiet' or 'No Cameras'. Little did I know how much more was involved behind the scenes. From 1999 to 2019, I had experience of working as a volunteer at golf's highest level and many of my memories are recounted within these pages.

Over the years, I had been keeping an A4 sized plastic folder (see illustration below) with special photographs and items such as my allocation of duties at The Ryder Cup Matches. While browsing through it one day, I had the inspiration to tie it all together and write this book. After all, I have heard people say that we all have at least one book in us – and this is mine. It is a privilege to share my experiences with you and I hope you enjoy reading about them.

I trust that my stories will appeal to golfers at all levels as well as anyone who likes to read about an ordinary person mixing with sporting legends at their place of work. To help keep 'my feet on the ground', I have added in some personal memories of the sport of golf 'outside the ropes' – in other words, the various friendships, and wonderful experiences I have enjoyed throughout my life in golf.

The first photograph (alongside) just has to be one taken with my very good friends in Budleigh Salterton when we played two or three times a year for the sheer fun of it. As we weren't members of any golf club at the time, we used to travel to Tiverton Golf Club which was happy to have visitors without the need to show handicap certificates. In those early days, Dr Graham Taylor made up the four – he was a fellow Scot from Stirling and I still see him when I return to Budleigh Salterton for the Lions Club Charity Golf Days. On our first visit to Tiverton, I happened to be wearing a white roll neck shirt under a dark blue jumper which made my appearance seem rather clerical to the lovely woman who signed us in, and she referred to us thereafter as 'The Vicars".

The pairings were generally formed with Bernard Brace and me on opposing sides – he was the most competitive of our group and I'll never forget his cheesy grin when my partner, David Low, missed a tap-in putt which should have in fairness been conceded! The only time I came near to beating Bernard was at Exeter Golf and Country Club when we were all square at the final hole and my ball was on the green in three. Bernard hit his third shot from off the green and the ball travelled across the green at about 20 miles per hour, hit the flag dead centre and dropped into the hole! Golf can be such a cruel sport.

Sadly, both David Low and Bernard Brace have since passed away and I know that they would have loved to have seen their photograph in print, no matter what the quality. Peter took the place of Dr Graham Taylor. We had such good times together – very competitive and nary a putt conceded unless it would otherwise topple into the hole unaided!

Someone once said – "Golf is like sex; you don't need to be good at it to enjoy it!"

David Low, Bernard Brace, Doug and Peter Fletcher

My original plastic folder with details of events and articles written for my local golf club – Henbury, BRISTOL

As a bit of background, I have played golf since the age of fourteen when I learned to play at a cliff-top links course in the North-East of Scotland – Strathlene Buckie Golf Club – which is one of the oldest golf courses in Scotland. It was perhaps this early introduction to the joys of links golf which, of course, is played throughout the United Kingdom on some of the finest links courses in the world, which eventually attracted me to volunteering at The Open Championship. I recently visited Buckie and took this aerial image of the course.

Strathlene Buckie Golf Club – with Findochty in the top right of the picture

Although I represented my school a couple of times, I didn't really take golf seriously until I moved to Wales in 1985, where I joined Southerndown Golf Club (described as a downland/links course), and I had the pleasure of winning my first ever trophy in 1992. I won The Rabbits Cup (for players with a handicap of eighteen or over) despite starting with an eleven on the first hole!

The story of that round of golf has been replayed more times than I care to mention. Enough to say that I scored 11, 10, 9, 8 on the first four holes, having hit out of bounds twice on the first hole! My playing partner on the day suggested that I calm down and simply enjoy the golf for the remaining fourteen holes. I calmed down so much that I parred all fourteen remaining holes and won the cup. The core of my performance was single putting no less than eight of the remaining holes – a feat that totally amazed my playing partner who couldn't believe the transformation. I don't know where that golf came from, but it has stayed hidden for the rest of my golfing life, apart from my putting ability which seems to have been built into my golfing brain!

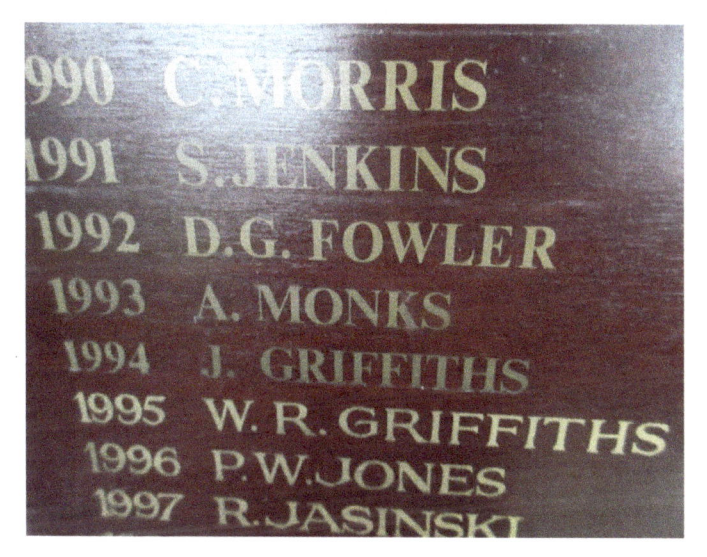

1992 Winner – Doug Fowler

Shortly after I joined Southerndown Golf Club, the Club Secretary wrote to all members asking them to support the club by attending The Duncan Putter Competition which is an amateur 72-hole competition held over a bank holiday weekend in April each year. Amateur players would be competing for, not only the trophy, but also early season ranking points in the Welsh Order of Merit, and it gives International and Walker Cup selectors a chance to assess early season form. Being a keen new member, I duly turned up early on the Sunday morning to watch the action. The response to members hadn't been too successful as I found that the 'spectators' amounted to the Club Captain, the Club Secretary and me along with any visiting spectators who came along to support their club's player. As all the amateur players arrived on the first tee, I was fascinated to note that they all had caddies and some even had golf bags on trollies. (Names such as Bradley Dredge and Gary Wolstenholme caught my eye as I had read about them in the golf magazines. Both went on the win the Duncan Putter in later years with Gary Wolstenholme winning it three times).

I watched each player tee off and gave all good tee shots a hearty round of applause – which sounded quite weird when the crowd is in single figures! The last pairing to step on the tee included a golfer from Rhyl, North Wales, and he had no caddie, so he was carrying his own clubs. His name was Tim Leah and he hit a magnificent drive down the middle of the fairway. I just couldn't stand by and watch him pick up his clubs, so I offered to carry his bag for him. It was a spur of the moment decision. Tim was somewhat surprised but grateful for the offer. So, I immediately became a caddie!

I made it clear to Tim, as we were walking up the first fairway, that I was a high handicap player so I wouldn't be able to offer him any advice. He just smiled, saying – "But you know the course and that will be very helpful!"

It was a real thrill to walk with a scratch golfer (zero handicap) on a course with which I was somewhat familiar. Tim played really well and hit almost every green 'in regulation' – one shot for a Par 3, two shots for a Par 4. In fact, he won a prize for the best front nine holes, going out in just 29 strokes. When we returned to the clubhouse for lunch, Tim had to bolt down a quick meal as he would be out on the first tee within half an hour. He asked me if I was available in the afternoon, and I said that I'd be happy to walk with him again. He said – "If you don't mind, can I choose the club when we get on the tee?" I was surprised at this question as I had been handing him his driver each time he got to the tee (apart from the Par 3s obviously) – as I had seen caddies do for their players when I had watched golf on the television. He then pointed out that he would not have used the driver on every hole that morning, but he decided to just 'go for it' each time as soon as I handed him the club! I felt so embarrassed that I had been so presumptive, and I sensed that my stint as a caddie was going to be short lived!

However, Tim just laughed it off and we gulped down our lunch before heading off to the tee in good time for his second round. He didn't play quite so well in the second round, but I put that down to the fact that he interfered with my club selection on his behalf! Unfortunately, I wasn't available to join him again on the second day's play as my wife had planned a visit to see my in-laws which was a shame as I would have loved to have completed the job for Tim.

I received a letter from Tim a few weeks later in which he thanked me for my services and asked if I was available to caddie for him at another competition in North Wales a few weeks later but I couldn't make that date either. Nevertheless, I had so enjoyed being a caddie and it gave me an insight into how valuable the caddie can be to a professional golfer, albeit that my experience had been at amateur level. It was also a great compliment that Tim had asked me to caddie for him again. My experience made me more aware of the top caddies and how hard they work during a round of golf, particularly in wet weather when they have to keep all the equipment dry and hold an umbrella for their player.

Team photograph of our Cardiff Architect's Office v firm of Quantity Surveyors in Cardiff (on the right) Our team is on the left: Doug, Tom, Steve (sadly no longer with us) and Russ

My only other experience of 'competitive golf' was when I was working in an architect's office in Cardiff, and we formed a team of four and we played against a team from a local quantity surveyor's practice. I can't remember the exact score but I'm pretty sure that we won the day! In our team of four, Russ Lewis was a student at the time (1986) and I was not to see him again until a chance meeting on the 10th Tee at The Belfry during the 2002 Ryder Cup Matches when he was surprised to see me 'inside the ropes' – more of that later.

Back to the journey I started with my introduction to the world of golf volunteering. After leaving Cardiff to work in Birmingham, one Monday morning in 1999, I asked my P.A. (Personal Assistant), Jayne, exactly what her partner did when he went off marshalling at the weekends and she briefly outlined his role. I remember saying something along the lines of, "That sounds really interesting, and I'd like to do that."

Within a couple of months, I was heading for my first experience of a professional golf tournament. From that day on, I filled my diary with as many of these adventures as I possibly could. Thus, began what I can only describe as a fabulous journey which, when I outline my experiences to golfing people, the question generally asked is, "How did you get into that?!"

I was to become heavily involved in experiencing the development of scoring systems within the game of golf at The Open Championship, where the golfing world demanded more and more information in respect of players' performances and the equipment they used. It is a revelation to discover exactly what goes on behind the television screen leader boards, which are such an integral part of following golf worldwide nowadays.

In the early days of my involvement with scoring, our duties were simply an integral part of reporting scores to the paying public through the use of leader boards strategically located around the golf course. The scoring systems became more and more sophisticated and demanded a high level of concentration to ensure that accurate information was recorded. This was essential as the information was beamed to all corners of the world in 'real time'.

I find that golfing friends, and people in general, are intrigued to hear 'the inside track' on such adventures, particularly when the names of top players are sprinkled into the mix. Hopefully, my experiences may resonate with most golfers, no matter what their ability or handicap. A friend once told me to "never let the truth get in the way of a good story", but my tales are true, otherwise there would be no point in my book. Besides which, most of the people mentioned are still around to take issue with my interpretation or memory of what happened.

I hope you enjoy this unique journey, as told by a golfer who has only broken 80 once in his life!

CHAPTER 1 – THE ENGLISH OPEN (1999)
The journey begins:

This story begins in the Midlands when I was working as an architect in Birmingham. Jayne was my P.A. and our Monday mornings usually started with a quick summary of our experiences of the previous weekend. Jayne often commented on the fact that she had been a 'golf widow' on Saturday and Sunday because her partner, Mick, had been at a golf tournament where he acted as a volunteer marshal.

As I said in the Introduction, that is where my thoughts turned to applying for such a role and being a switched-on woman, Jayne duly obliged by getting hold of one of Mick's application forms before deleting his information so that I could enter my own details over the information that had been hidden by several layers of Tipp-Ex. My first application form was sent out on 12th December 1999 when I applied to act as a marshal at The English Open, which was being held at the Forest of Arden Golf Club in June 2000.

Jayne was later to tell me that Mick had had a bit of a reprimand for copying the form because the organisers liked to control new applications themselves. However, I later learned that my keenness was considered invaluable as it showed a determination and use of initiative, both the hallmarks of a good volunteer marshal.

One of the tick boxes on the application form was a question asking if I was prepared to assist with 'on-course' scoring and the use of a radio if required. Having never used a radio on-course before, I ticked the box on the basis that, as my grandson Elliot says, "If you don't ask, you don't get!" and little did I realise how much this simple action would change my golf volunteering involvement in the future and take me to the highest level of golf at major tournaments such as The Open Championship and Ryder Cup Matches.

I will never forget the excitement of receiving a letter indicating that my application was successful; I had to report to the Chief Marshal on Thursday 1st June 2000, a red-letter day in my golfing diary as well as my brother Ian's birthday.

Thankfully, the Forest of Arden Golf Club was reasonably accessible on a daily basis from my home at the time in Droitwich Spa and, therefore, there was no need for me to book accommodation near the course. The need to arrange our own accommodation was to become a major issue when arranging my availability to volunteer, as will be described later. Whilst the European Tour officials were generous in giving marshals good quality outfits to wear and luncheon vouchers to feed them, volunteers had to bear all other expenses. I recall thinking at the time that I would happily pay for the privilege of working "inside the ropes" because I would get to see top golfers close at hand. It was a privilege that I never lost sight of throughout my experiences outlined in this book.

From the very outset I took photographs of players and celebrities whenever it was appropriate to do so but never on competition days when we were instructed to have no communications with the players. I still cringe when I hear youngsters calling out to players in the middle of their round and even worse after the round is complete when they would ask for items of clothing. On one occasion, I even heard a young boy ask a player if he could have his golf clubs! It was quite normal for the player and/or caddie to throw golf balls into the crowd of spectators around the eighteenth green on completion of their round.

Doug with the late Eduardo Romero

Doug with Simon Dyson

I use the term "inside the ropes" as all golf tournaments would ensure a clear space for golfers by roping off areas where the spectators could stand and view the action. To work within those enclosures was limited to only a few. It would be fair to say that working within the ropes was hard work but worth every minute in terms of job satisfaction.

Other than the players and their caddies, it was mainly officials and media people including cameramen and sound engineers who held what looked like furry animals masking their microphones. (The covering of the microphones allowed sounds to be picked up without wind noises obliterating the noise, or should I say sweet sound, made when a golf club connected with a golf ball. When watching golf on the television, one can normally see these sound recordist technicians hovering around the players in order to direct their microphones as stealthily as possible).

On Thursday 1st June, I travelled to the golf course by car, arriving just before 6am and I found that the allocated car parking area was already filling up with volunteers. I parked up and changed into my golf shoes before joining the throng of marshals walking towards the Marshals' Headquarters. Even in the car park, there was an air of excitement amongst those changing into their golf shoes before heading on to the course. It seemed like a large family gathering as so many of the volunteers already knew each other. After all, they were mainly chosen from golf clubs in the locality.

At the HQ, I was greeted by Barry Drew, Chief Marshal for the European Tour, a lovely gentleman sporting a smart green blazer and a cap with the words 'CHIEF MARSHAL' in large letters across the brim. He had a very military bearing and I wondered if he had been in the services.

Barry shook my hand vigorously and said, "I've been looking forward to meeting you. We like people who are keen," before he guided me towards a chattering queue of marshals where a mix of young and old were lining up to receive their duties for the day. I'll never forget the excitement levels that were displayed by all present.

They were all shuffling forward towards a large desk where I noticed a very capable-looking woman, with spectacles perched on the end of her button nose, calling out instructions to various people within the room. This was Mavis Drew, Barry's wife, and she spoke with a very thick Brummie accent. On a desk in front of her, Mavis had a giant spreadsheet – in the days before I had experience of Microsoft Excel – which was a large cardboard sheet ruled off in a very neat format with colour-coded responsibilities that were to be allocated to the volunteers as they approached the front of the queue. Mavis was affectionately known as "MAM" which actually stood for "Marshals Administration Manager", and she certainly could manage.

As an architect, I appreciated the technical brilliance of the straight lines, which had been drawn with mechanical precision. A thing of beauty as well as a working tool, which was filled in with names and hieroglyphics at an amazing speed as people were 'processed'. I never ceased to be totally in awe of Mavis's unswerving ability to coordinate the activities of all the volunteers, most of whom she already knew by first name.

Barry Drew – Chief Marshal and his wife, Mavis, known as "MAM" (Marshals Administration Manager)

"Welcome. Pleased to meet you," she said as she scanned her spreadsheet for my name which was then highlighted with an orange highlighter marker pen. She handed me a slip of paper with a name on it, 'Graham Faulkner', who I was to learn was a Senior Marshal in charge of a zone on the golf course.

The course was divided up into zones with a Senior Marshal in charge of a group of about forty or fifty volunteers who would be responsible for crowd control duties out on the course. That was my guess when I saw the assembled group outside later. Graham handed me lunch vouchers, which I soon found out could be exchanged for golf equipment in the pro shop, and a small booklet entitled 'Marshal's Handbook' that contained all the information that I would require to fulfil my duties as a marshal. Speed-reading was required to get the gist of what was required and, *'Why didn't they send this to me beforehand?'* went through my mind but, as a newcomer, I decided that discretion was the best option, and I never asked the question.

I was then directed to another queue where I was to receive my outfit for the week. I recalled filling out the application form and choosing the XL size of shirt and protective jacket. I sincerely hoped these items would fit my ever-expanding waistline. Two assistant marshals reached into giant cardboard boxes behind them to retrieve the requisite items listed against my name.

When I say 'outfit', it was two shirts, a waterproof jacket, and a cap – all bearing the logo of the sponsors of the event. The 'gear' was good quality and we had been advised to wear dark trousers – I chose black – to complete the outfit. It felt good to change into the shirt and don the jacket; I felt like a proper marshal and headed over to an assembling group to be briefed on my duties for the day. Suddenly, I was part of the team and it felt good.

It was clear that quite a few of the other volunteers were experienced and knew each other well. It didn't take me long to get chatting to a few marshals, most of whom were from the Birmingham area judging by the accents I heard on that first morning. I quickly learned the hierarchy within the marshals' world – it's always good to know where you stand.

Graham called out names; he was sub-dividing his marshals into smaller groups for on-course management and I was told that I would be working on Holes 9 and 10, which I later appreciated as there was a food station nearby. 'Yum Yum's' was run by a couple of lovely women called Michelle and Julie. They knew many of the marshals who visited their stand daily and their hot dogs were legendary. In fact, they turned up at quite a few other venues and I got to know them well as a result. They were always a welcome sight first thing in the morning as they passed out hot cups of coffee to the gathering crowd of marshals who swarmed around their wagon like bees round a honeypot.

Doug kitted up with marshal's uniform

Michelle and Julie at YumYum's

The briefing was short and I realised straight away that I was going to be relied on to use my common sense when working on the course – simple things like "don't stand in the line of a player putting on the green" and "don't get in front of the television cameras" (as Barry had said, "You're not here to be TV celebrities!" and that was in the days before the words 'TV' and 'celebrity' were to become inexorably linked). Being a golfer who was very keen on etiquette and courtesy, I found most of the volunteer rules to be second nature.

Before I knew it, I was called to board a minibus, which took our group out to Hole 9 where I was handed a 'KEEP QUIET' board and told to have a good day. That was it; no further instructions, and I didn't see Graham again that morning.

I should explain that the 9th Hole at the Forest of Arden Golf Club is a Par 3 over a pond from a tee that I could see between some trees in the middle distance. The time was now approaching 8am when the public were allowed on to the course, so I was really excited at meeting the first of the spectators who were arriving to find their favourite spot. Having strolled round the green a couple of times, I noticed a woman who was settling in to watch the ensuing action.

I wandered over to her and introduced myself, saying something along the lines of, "It's my job to keep you under control."

She immediately quipped, "I am seventy-six and nobody has ever been able to control me!" We had a laugh together and I realised then how much spectators like to communicate with us 'officials'. I never lost that connection with spectators as it imbues the spirit of togetherness, which the love of golf engenders.

During my first two hours by the green, only a handful of spectators gathered around, so keeping order was quite simple even though I was on my own. Suddenly, I was aware of a huge crowd walking alongside the 8th fairway to my left – it was a formidable three-ball featuring Michael Campbell, Darren Clarke and Lee Westwood – Campbell was on 8 under on his first round! I should explain that he had started on the 10th tee as the tournament had a '2 Tee Start' which was quite normal, to increase the number of players on the course. TV cameras were everywhere, and activity levels suddenly seemed to increase rapidly. Shots played were greeted by loud applause, so I knew that something special was in the air. Perhaps Michael Campbell was on his way to the holy grail of scoring a sub 60 round? The atmosphere in the place was buzzing.

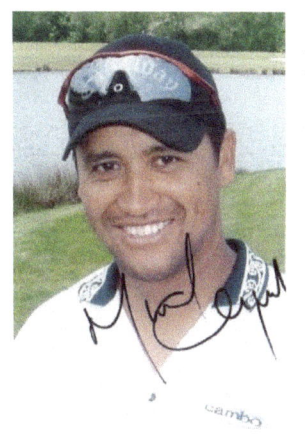

Michael Campbell   Darren Clarke OBE

Lee Westwood

Before I knew it, the crowd was three or four deep all around the green as Campbell prepared to tee off on the 9th Hole.

His shot landed in the front of the green, dead centre. Lee Westwood pulled his tee shot left into some bushes by the green – I made a note of where his ball ended up. Next on the tee was Darren Clarke who pushed his tee shot off to the right, also ending up in some bushes. As the group started walking towards the green, I realised that I had better find the players' golf balls that had ended up in the bushes. Having found where Lee Westwood's ball was located – in an unplayable lie under a thick bush – I took off my cap and placed it nearby as a marker for Lee when he got close to the spot. It was a brand-new cap and I hoped that I would get it back.

Noticing that the players were about fifty yards away and advancing at a steady pace, I set off across the green to find Darren Clarke's ball when I heard a loud voice shouting, "Get off the bloody green!"

I turned round to see Barry Drew, the Chief Marshal, on his buggy. He had a megaphone device in his hand and his voice carried right across the course. I felt so embarrassed that my complexion flushed bright red.

He had come to check on me. With a sinking heart – after all it was my first day as a marshal – I started to explain to Barry that Darren Clarke would be very unhappy if I didn't find his ball for him, but that didn't exonerate me. I had committed the cardinal sin of venturing on to the hallowed turf. Even with golf shoes on, that was not allowed, as I found out to my embarrassment. I envisaged the shortest ever career in marshalling coming to an end right soon.

As it was, Darren Clarke and his caddie took several minutes to find his ball because all I could do was point vaguely to where I thought it had landed; he was not a happy man. Neither was Barry. I had managed to upset two people in the space of as many minutes. I never walked on a green again – Lesson No.1.

The rest of the morning was uneventful, but I enjoyed chatting to spectators in between action on the green. It was lovely to find out where people were from and discover what level of golf they played at, with most being a lower handicap than me, being a member of Gaudet Luce Golf

Club with a handicap of 24! Also, I had the privilege of seeing quite a few famous golfers close at hand. I soon discovered how approachable these golfers were, provided one respected their concentration on tournament days when they would be 'in the zone'. I often saw other marshals invade that level of privacy and I would wince at their ineptitude.

At noon, my Senior Marshal turned up and advised me that I should take a break of one hour after which my duties would transfer to ball spotting on the nearby 10th Hole, which was a Par 4. Out came my lunch vouchers and I had one of the tastiest burgers I can ever recall - from YumYum's, with chips of course. I also chatted to a few of my fellow marshals – a lovely group of friendly individuals who took to me quite quickly. I am a gregarious type, if I say so myself, and always enjoy engaging with new people whenever I get an opportunity. I could hear several marshals talking about the 2001 Ryder Cup Matches and how excited they were at the prospect of marshalling at such a prestigious event, which was to be held nearby at The Belfry, Sutton Coldfield.

I had my ear to the ground and wondered what chance I would have of joining their ranks, albeit I was such a novice marshal. Later that day, a conversation with John Wardle, the Senior Scoring Marshal, was to significantly change my golf volunteering life, but little did I know it at the time.

It was almost a casual conversation when John introduced himself to me and asked if I could operate an on-course radio. Having never done so, I answered, "Yes," and he made a note of my name then moved on his way. I wasn't going to miss out on the opportunity of a lifetime and how difficult could it be to operate a radio?

When John realised that I was Scottish, his conversation immediately turned to his love of single malt whisky, his favourite being Benromach, with which I was unfamiliar.

However, I was to check it out when I next visited my folks in Scotland, and I was fascinated to enjoy a tour round one of the smallest ever whisky distilleries, which had only one operative who was all job descriptions rolled into one. Indeed, I often wondered if John's mention of his favourite single malt was a ruse to get me to buy him a bottle, so I bought a miniature for him during my visit to the distillery in Elgin, a town only eighteen miles away from my hometown of Buckie which is on the Moray Firth, sixty miles north-west of Aberdeen.

Before my discussion with John Wardle, my ball-spotting duties started on Hole 10, which was a 'one sided hole' in terms of on-course marshalling. In other words, spectators were only located on one side of the fairway to the left, the other side being part of the forest after which the course was named. My instructions were to stand by the trees at approximately 250 yards from the tee so that I could spot any stray shots that headed toward the trees which were not 'out of bounds'. Barry Drew and his team liked to ensure that players were given every assistance in smoothing their passage around the golf course.

Using a pair of binoculars, I watched players as they teed off and a marshal, standing immediately behind the tee, would signal the direction of the shot using his 'Keep Quiet' board as a pointer. An up and down signal indicated a drive that was 'right down the middle'. Similarly, a lean to the right indicated a slice while a lean to the left was a hook. It always amused me when golfing friends would describe their slices as 'fades' and their hooks as 'draws'.

The first player to hit a ball in my direction was the late, great Seve Ballesteros! Imagine my excitement as he approached where I was standing. Having found his ball in a decent lie on the right-hand side of the fairway, I gestured towards the ball and stepped back out of his way. My heart was beating with excitement as I realised how close I was to an icon of the game and three-times winner of The Open Championship and who was standing just a few feet away from me.

He came right up to me and thanked me for locating his ball; he was so gracious and charming, with that infectious smile. He was a most handsome man. I just glowed with pleasure, having spoken to my golfing hero on my very first day as a marshal. Seve took dead aim and hit a majestic shot up near the green. He tipped his cap in thanks as he walked away and along the fairway. Shortly after he walked away, my heart was still beating powerfully, and my chest had expanded by several inches with the excitement of it all.

No sooner had Seve gone on his way than a photographer – wearing kneepads and with several cameras hanging from his neck – came across the fairway and asked me what I was doing. He seemed really agitated and I wondered what had happened to enrage him so.

Puzzled, I told him that I was there to spot balls and he moaned about the fact that he was trying to take a picture of Seve, but I was standing right there in the background. Telling him that his photo would probably, therefore, make it into the next edition of *Golf Monthly* didn't improve his demeanour! He shuffled off muttering as he went, and I noted that he was to be avoided if I came across him on the course again.

Despite the slight contretemps with the photographer, the rest of day was a joy as I was moved around to various parts of Hole 10, and I met so many lovely spectators as well as seeing some top players up close and personal. Spectators generally enjoyed chatting to an 'official' inside the ropes as it helped with the overall communications, and they asked questions all the time. Even general marshalling duties demanded a constant state of alertness. For example, if a player hit his ball outside the ropes, it was our responsibility to lower the ropes and allow the player easy access to his ball. In my short time as a marshal, I had seen other marshals fail to do this and the player or caddie had to lift the ropes themselves, a situation that was not acceptable in my book.

Whenever I watch golf on the television, I look closely for the marshals to see if they are observing the etiquette of kneeling down when shots are being played so that the spectators' view is not blocked. It is, unfortunately, a common problem to see marshals standing watching the action whereas their job is to watch the crowd. When admission prices are not cheap, it is really unforgivable for marshals to be standing in the way of the paying public and I always communicated with spectators as well as positioning myself to ensure that they could see past my great bulk.

As part of the 'hole rotation' I was moved back up to the tee for a period. Standing behind the tee on Hole 10, I was surprised to see Darren Clarke run his driver up the inside leg of Lee Westwood's trousers just as he was addressing his ball. I was rather shocked to witness that because I'd think twice about pulling a stunt like that with one of my golfing buddies let alone doing it in the middle of a golf tournament. It was a measure of how friendly these two players were at that time as I was to witness on several occasions. Anyway, Lee hit his drive right down the middle, clearly unfazed by Darren's prank.

Later that day, after I had finished my duties, I hung around the practice putting green and I was watching Paul Broadhurst working with some extraordinary contraption that seemed to guide his putter head along a straight line when I noticed that Seve had come back out to practise there as well. I waited patiently as I didn't want to be one of those spectators who would shout across at the players in their attempts to get autographs.

When I saw Seve move towards the exit from the putting area, I managed to manoeuvre myself alongside him and said, "Mr Ballesteros, hello again. May I have your autograph, please?"

Thankfully, he seemed to recognise me from our earlier encounter, probably because I was six foot four, and he obligingly signed my programme. I didn't have my camera at the ready and that was one of the biggest regrets of my golfing life. I realised there wouldn't be too many opportunities to get close to such an icon of the game and so it transpired that I never did again before he passed away ten years later. I have a vivid memory of one of the finest golfers that ever lived and my meetings with him twice in one day.

When I returned to the marshals' compound, John Wardle asked me if I would help with scoring on the following day as he was short of scoring marshals. I agreed instantly and he introduced me to Peter Houghton, his deputy. Peter had a shaven head and wore a large earring; he also had a very thick Brummie accent. On initially meeting him, I thought that he looked like a skinhead! How wrong could I be? Peter told me that my job would simply be to stand by the exit of a green and obtain the players' scores for that hole. Instructions would be given the following day when I arrived at the course. My excitement levels were elevated even higher as I looked forward to the next day's duties.

**John Wardle –
Senior Scoring
Marshal**

**Peter Houghton –
John's deputy**

Within 24 hours, I had progressed from an on-course marshal to being part of the scoring team and that is where I spent the rest of my volunteering days. By the end of my first day, I had already befriended a few marshals who were to become close friends over the ensuing years.

As I was leaving the course at the end of a wonderful day, the route to the car park was via the driving range and there was Lee Westwood, cutting a solitary figure, hitting golf ball after golf ball. His dedication to practising was universally regarded as one of his defining qualities. All the sadder that he hasn't yet won a major golf tournament although he has had a great career in golf and played a major role in several Ryder Cup Matches over the years. As clarification for non-golfers, the majors are The Masters Tournament, The US Open, The Open Championship and the PGA Championship – The Open being considered THE event to win and the only one played in the United Kingdom, the others being played in America.

CHAPTER 2 (2000) THE ENGLISH OPEN

Peter Fowler with Doug   Peter Fowler's autograph

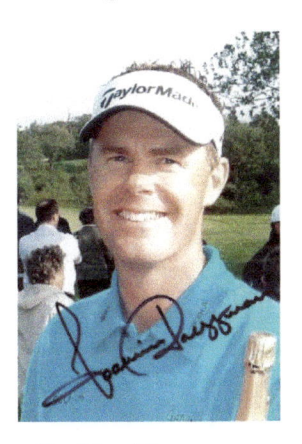

Joakim Haeggman

One of the first players that I encountered on the course was Peter Fowler – namesake of one of my cousins. I asked if I could have a photograph taken with him as he was not only a Fowler, but he was taller than me. I also came across Joakim Haeggman, the first Swedish player to play in The

Ryder Cup Matches. He was very friendly and always happy to pose for photographs or sign autographs. So began my unique collection of players' photographs which I treasure to this day.

Having progressed from marshal to being part of the scoring team, I turned up on Day 2 with even more excitement than on Day 1. As I am an early riser – my father was a baker who owned his own business and I spent most of my schooldays working in his bakery before going to school in the morning – I was one of the first to arrive in the Marshals' Headquarters. Mavis looked me up and down and said, "You're keen!" She ticked me off her list and ushered me to the desk where John Wardle was sitting. He was deep in conversation with Pete Houghton and broke it off to welcome me with that engaging smile of his. John was an ex-teacher and one of the best man managers that I was to experience in my life. My relationship with John was to flourish and almost immediately he knew that he could trust me – a vital quality when dealing with players and their scores.

He greeted me with a firm handshake. "Let's get you started!"

That was about it as he handed me another handbook – '*Scoring Marshals' Handbook*'– to add to my small collection! He instructed me to collect my lunch vouchers and join him in a small group in the corner of the room where I was introduced to a fine body of men (who considered themselves the 'elite' marshal group, whereas I was to learn that most marshals thought of scoring as an 'easy job' requiring little in the way of brains or stamina!).

John outlined the process of scoring during the tournament; it involved sitting by the exit to a particular green, asking the players for their scores as they were walking off the green towards the next tee and then radioing their scores to 'Control'. John explained that an element of diplomacy was required in this respect as 'certain players' like Colin Montgomerie and Darren Clarke seemed to find this an intrusion, albeit they had signed up to the European Tour arrangements that included this very procedure. In those days, scoring was quite a simple process because all that was required was the number of strokes taken by each player at each hole; as long as that corresponded accurately with the card in the player's hand, all was perfect. In all honesty, I always found Colin Montgomerie and Darren Clarke to be perfectly reasonable people, it was just a case of being respectful to them when asking the question.

I was soon to devise a technique that avoided any confrontation and that was to ask the player that I didn't recognise – they played as 3-balls on the first two days – and he would give the score of the other two players. Another technique that I quickly assimilated was asking the player who had the best score on the hole as they were invariably happy to declare their success.

I need to clarify, at this point, that scoring marshals are in no way involved with the players' own scorecards as these are the responsibility solely of the players themselves and, once signed for, become the formal record of their score for all eighteen holes during their round of golf.

In those early days, there were no walking scoreboard carriers, and updated scores were relayed to Control from which they would be radioed out to a few leader boards that were positioned strategically around the course. I realise now how poor the information was from a spectator point of view because the presentation of scores was somewhat delayed before making it to the leader boards. Sometimes caddies would offer the scores, but I was advised that this was not the correct procedure, and I did incur the 'Darren Clarke hard stare' later that very day! When I asked him for his score, he simply grunted, "Ask my caddie." I assumed he was having a bad round.

As an aside, a few years later, when I was training a fellow scoring marshal in the art of asking the right player, we witnessed a French player, Jean-Francois Remesy, record a triple bogey (three over par) on a Par 4 Hole at Celtic Manor. I nudged my trainee and said, "Don't ask him, whatever you do!" With that, the player bounded up to our position, announced his name and said, "My name is Remesy, and I scored a seven!" almost triumphantly, as if he was pleased and he also quoted the other players' scores before marching off to the next tee. You just never can tell.

Armed with a short-band radio – which had several available bands, but I was instructed to use Band 1 – I headed off to my location by Hole 3. I was later to learn that Band 9 was a private line between The Chief Marshal and his team of Senior Marshals. Of course, I tuned in from time to time to hear what was really going on. As the radios came with an ill-fitting earpiece, it was important to control the volume of the radio so that no sounds 'leaked out' and disturbed players' concentration or came to the attention of nearby spectators. Having large ears, I had to seek out a larger than normal earpiece after I had endured a sore ear the first time I had worn the standard one. It was quite an art to thread the wire through my jacket and to the radio which was clipped to my waistband. Having once snagged the wire on a fence post, it tugged my ear which suffered tingling pain for hours afterwards.

Later in my scoring career, I had to perfect the way of turning up the sound to hear what was going on and remembering to turn the volume down as players were putting out. It took some time to get this balance right and, while the sound seemed extremely loud to me, I would ask some person nearby if they could hear what I was hearing. This balancing of activities was combined with the art of standing in the right place off the green so that I could see all the action and be well-placed to make it to the next tee along with the players, caddies, and match referee, etc.

Quite often I would trail behind the players and caddies much to the frustration of marshals who were holding back the crowd of spectators who wanted to cross a fairway or make it to another vantage point on the course.

I overheard some amusing exchanges when a new scoring marshal was radioing in scores and 'Control' would say, "Take your finger off the button when you've finished talking, over!" The movie *Airplane* would spring to mind, where the air traffic controller was called 'Over'. "Hole 6 to Control – over" was followed by silence as the culprit hadn't let go of the button. Such was the challenge facing the organisers on a regular basis as the employment of new radio users seemed to be quite common.

Also, to reduce the number of scoring marshals (probably because of too many incidents like the above – apparently quite a few were making mistakes and causing huge embarrassment), a more streamlined system was introduced whereby scoring marshals were located by every third green. We had to enquire of the players what scores had been logged for the current hole for each player and the two previous holes. I was always impressed how any player could always recount not only their own scores but those of the other players as well. The new system worked well as golf scores are normally recounted in sets of three – 443:543:445 – and so on.

'Control', the scoring central hub, was run by a tall, dark-haired gentleman called Lee. His ability to take in numerous scores from all over the course always impressed me. I recall standing behind him in his headquarters after one of my scoring stints and listening to his handling of the incoming scores. He transferred the information to his laptop spreadsheet and to the nearby press office. It was a masterpiece of precision information and reminded me of the spreadsheet that Mavis used. How would she cope with such a device, I wondered? I never asked her but undoubtedly she'd shrug it off saying that her system was better (and it usually was!).

Lee – Control Room Chief **Scorers receiving their radios and score sheets**

After all, the whole purpose of having scoring marshals was to communicate the scores of all players to spectators and the media, in that order, as many spectators (the paying public) would turn up at the course to perhaps follow their own favourite player or club professional in many instances. Of course, some players expressed an interest in other players' scores whereas most liked to ignore any outside factors that might inhibit their play when they were 'in the zone'. As my experience was to develop, scoring information was to take on a whole different slant whereby the media, and the public at large, would demand more detailed information such as which club the player used, the exact yardage of the drive, where the golf ball ended up, etc.

Of the many golfers that I encountered in the early days, a name that springs to mind is John Bickerton, who was a local professional at Redditch Golf Club and quite a few people were following him around the Forest of Arden when I was learning to score. I seemed to bump into John quite often. He was an immensely personable golfer who was always prepared to engage with the public. Our chance meetings became so frequent that he once asked me, "Are you stalking me?!" As a result of meeting him so often, I was able to choose my moment when to ask him if I could take his photograph. I followed his progress in a few events after that and was always pleased when he did well.

John Bickerton

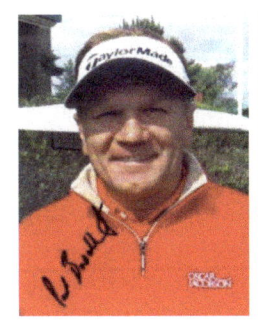

Paul Broadhurst **Paul Casey**

In terms of taking photographs of top professional golfers, early in my career as a marshal I decided that I would politely ask each player if I could take their photograph. When they consented, it meant that in that moment of pressing the shutter, I had an intimate connection with that player as they looked into my lens and I said – "Smile please". It also gave me a unique photograph which I would later – at some future tournament – ask them to sign, thereby rounding off the uniqueness of my photograph collection. All my photographs are therefore very personal, making them all the more important to me.

To get that 'one-to-one' moment, I generally arrived at the golf course early in the morning and would seek out players as they were heading to the driving range or putting green before the public were admitted to the course. In that way, players were more relaxed and willing to pose briefly for me to take their photograph. It was considered taboo to ask players who were on their way to the first tee on competition days, whereas the 'pro-celebrity' fun sessions on a Wednesday were ripe for such requests, albeit the main problem was that large numbers of spectators were after the same thing.

When I use the term 'top players' when referring to the European Tour at that time, notable names were Colin Montgomerie, Darren Clarke, Lee Westwood, and Seve Ballesteros. The latter was, at that time, in decline as many of the golfing press were observing. Nevertheless, Seve had an aura about him – probably the most loved golfer of all time if I'm honest. Certainly, when he passed away in 2011, The Open Championship was played at Royal St George's, Sandwich that year and the organisers put up huge images of Seve all along the entrance area together with tributes around the grandstands. I saw grown men and women, myself included, weep openly at the sadness of his untimely passing.

Throughout my career as a volunteer, I never managed to get photographs of Jack Nicklaus or Tom Watson, which was a shame as I admired them both in equal measure. I did, however, get Tom Watson to sign a tribute that I had prepared for a friend at The Open Championship at St Andrews in 2005. I have included a photograph of that item later in this book. I also sent a five-pound note to Jack Nicklaus in Florida for him to sign but he returned a photograph which he had signed (together with my five-pound note) with his best wishes.

David Howell    **Ian Poulter**

Graeme McDowell

I had the good fortune to meet many of the top European Tour players at that time, including David Howell, Ian Poulter and Graeme McDowell. They have all been involved in The Ryder Cup Matches and I had the thrill of walking with David in 2006 at The K Club. David Howell has to be one of the most approachable golfers on the tour and everyone I talked to about him agreed that he is a real gentleman.

Scoring, however, was my first love in terms of being a volunteer marshal and, in the first few days, the words on everyone's lips was "The Ryder Cup" which was being held locally at The Belfry the following year. As a beginner, I hesitated to approach John Wardle about being chosen to act as a scorer at such a prestigious event but imagine my sheer excitement at being told that I was 'in the running'. In fact, John sidled up to me one day and quietly said, "Doug, don't say anything but I am recommending you for our scoring team at the Ryder Cup Matches next year."

I could hardly contain myself at the thought of working in such an electric environment.

John added, "The atmosphere at the Ryder Cup Matches is different to any other golfing event as it is played in front of huge crowds that will be shouting for their respective teams. A bit like being on a football field in front of a crowd of forty thousand!"

Later in this book, I will mention my attempts to upgrade the standards of scoring at these European Tour events, but these were overshadowed by the sheer professionalism of the scoring processes used for The Open Championship, which is under the auspices of the R&A (Royal & Ancient Golf Club of St Andrews), who are custodians of the Rules of Golf. Their attention to detail is like a military operation with nothing left to chance. I first experienced this in 2006 when I did my first stint as a Walking Scorer at The Open Championship – a job that involved recording every single shot played by each player throughout their round, just as in the Ryder Cup Matches in 2002. After all, scores are the lifeblood of any reporting on tournaments and the communication of these is vital to the success of any press release.

Mentioning the Rules of Golf, it is a book that all golfers should read no matter what their playing level. Over the years, I have been amazed at how ignorant many club golfers are about the rules and I am quite convinced that many break them without ever realising it!

The Introduction states – *"Play the ball as it lies, play the course as you find it, and if you cannot do either, do what is fair. But to do what is fair, you need to know the Rules of Golf."*

On the very next page a Rolex advert states – *"One Game: For over 500 years golf has provided an endless allure for competitive and recreational golfers alike. Its challenge and camaraderie bring out the best in all participants and creates a genuine and lasting pact among those who play. Its mastery is a lifelong pursuit."* Sage words.

One final point about the Rules of Golf – when wondering about the correct way to spell 'caddie' (sometimes spelt 'caddy'), I turned to the Definitions section which states that "Caddie – a 'caddie' is one who assists the player in accordance with the Rules, which may include carrying or handling the player's clubs during play."

In this first year as a marshal, I also worked as a 'spotter' at the PGA Seniors Championship, which was played at The Belfry on the PGA National Course. Standing to the right-hand side of a Par 5, I was ball spotting in the light rough when Maurice Bembridge's ball landed near me. His was a name that I had heard before so there was an additional air of excitement at seeing him close by.

Maurice came striding up to his ball, thanked me for my assistance and started a discussion with his caddie. He decided to play a 3-wood out of the rough as his lie was quite friendly. Taking dead aim, he swung his club and made a perfect contact with the ball, which flew straight into a slender sapling about ten yards in front of him. The ball ricocheted back towards him and landed about two yards behind where he was standing.

He looked straight at me and asked, "What do you think of that?"

I had to keep a straight face and muttered something along the lines of the fact that it was very bad luck! I'll never forget his calm demeanour as he placed the 3-wood back into his golf bag, scratched his head and then took out the same club again. He reckoned that it was just bad luck with his second shot and took dead aim again. This time, after a swish of the club, he made a perfect contact and the ball arrowed its way on to the green, ending up about five feet from the flag. He would be putting for birdie.

It was an object lesson in keeping one's composure in adversity! Maurice went on to finish second in the tournament with a score of ten under par.

Later that same day, I found myself with a small group of marshals who were on a break from a nearby feeding station. They reckoned that ball spotting as a group would result in less balls being lost, not that we had lost any at that point in the day. Speaking too soon, we heard a thud behind us, and we started searching for the ball which had just been hit by the then leader of the tournament. So, there was an air of panic as the Senior Marshal, standing close by, signalled back to the player to the effect that the ball had not been found, on the basis that he would then have the opportunity to play a provisional ball. The player – whose name I forget – who was leading the tournament at the time, came striding up to our position pointing to some water just beyond, saying that his ball had gone in the water. To a man, we said that it hadn't as we'd heard it thump into the ground behind us where the grass was quite long.

Nevertheless, the player carried on a few yards and declared that, as his ball had been lost in a water hazard, he could have a drop behind it. With that, he dropped a ball and played a shot on to the green. We stood there open-mouthed but realised that the player probably knew better. The Senior Marshal said that something wasn't right about that incident, and he went to the Referee's Office to make a statement about what had just happened. The officials took the report seriously and ordered the player to return to the spot where we were standing and explain his side of things. The Senior Marshal pointed to the rough area where he thought the player's golf ball had landed but the player continued to dispute what he was saying, maintaining that his ball had gone into the water just ahead. The referee suddenly stood on a ball, and, on examination, it was indeed found to be the player's 'lost in the water ball' with its distinctive mark on it. He was disqualified immediately. I only heard the conclusion to this story when I met up with the Senior Marshal later in the day.

This just goes to show that the game of golf can involve tricky situations where players' interpretation of the Rules of Golf can be questioned albeit that is the purview of the Match Referees, not the marshals. I have often been asked if I have been posed a question by a player when it comes to a rules interpretation, but that never happened as our instructions were to always call for a Referee if there was any doubt about a penalty drop or the like. Indeed, the rules officials carried a very thick book of 'Rules Decisions' just in case they were faced with an awkward situation.

CHAPTER 3 (2001)
THE WALES OPEN

The Wales Open (not to be known as The Welsh Open – unlike the English and Scottish counterparts) was played early in the year, normally at the end of March, so it was my first stint of volunteering in 2001. This was only the second year of its staging, the first having been won by Steen Tinning in 2000.

Played at Celtic Manor, it was quite accessible to me, just a short drive across the Severn Estuary as I was living in Bristol at the time. Here I met a remarkable bunch of volunteers with whom I was to enjoy many happy times. Sir Terry Matthews – owner of Celtic Manor – was a very generous sponsor of the event and marshals were each given a voucher to play the course after the event. It was always a delight, no matter what standard of golf I played, to play the holes that I had watched the professionals on shortly before. Indeed, Sir Terry worked tirelessly to bring top golf to Wales, and he was successful in securing The Ryder Cup in 2010 – a fantastic achievement for golf in Wales.

**Doug, Nick, Mike and Jim before our
complimentary round at Westwood Hills Course**

The Chief Marshal and his team had their headquarters in a large building just beyond the first tee (the driving range). Our allocated car parking was close to the hotel, and we were taken by minibus to our headquarters thereafter. The location was perfect as we were able to watch the golfers practising nearby when we were not carrying out our duties on the course. I recall one practice day when Paul Casey gave a masterclass of how to hit a variety of shots off the tee. He was wired up and gave a running commentary of how he hit various 'fades' (left-to-right shot) and 'draws' (right-to-left shot). I was fascinated to see how well he controlled the flight of a golf ball over such enormous distances. One look at the size of his forearms was a clue to part of his secret.

Barry, Mavis, and their Senior Marshals had a well-oiled operation whereby duties were allocated to volunteers when they arrived before they received their complimentary clothing, emblazoned with the familiar Welsh dragon. I had already met many of the Welsh volunteers at my previous events and there was a strong sense of camaraderie amongst us.

The Wentwood Hills course was one of three at the resort along with the Montgomerie and Roman Road. The course was effectively on two levels with a drop of about 100 feet after an opening Par 5 hole of over 500 yards. We were 'buggied' out to our various positions on the course generally amidst a buzz of chatter and banter along the way. Again, I was part of the scoring team and thoroughly enjoyed my time in this part of the countryside in Wales. The golf course is located on the north-side of Christchurch Hill running down to the River Usk – very picturesque. Most of the marshals were Welsh from surrounding golf clubs and I felt really at home amongst this band of Celts.

The event was won by Paul McGinley in a play-off with Darren Lee and Paul Lawrie.

Paul McGinley

Paul Lawrie OBE

CHAPTER 4 (2002)
THE GREAT NORTH OPEN, THE ENGLISH OPEN & THE RYDER CUP (THE BELFRY):

2002 was a great year for me and it started on 11th February when I scored my first hole-in-one at the 13th Hole at Henbury Golf Club. A majestic 8-iron that never left the pin and I recall the oddly strange feeling of watching the ball disappear into the hole. I say my first hole-in-one not because I have ever repeated the feat but golf develops a positive frame of mind in high handicap golfers.

My bar bill was £68.74 – it was a tradition to buy everyone in the clubhouse a drink on such an illustrious occasion. Indeed, I was so thrilled that I even checked out the snooker room at the club to ensure that members in there could avail themselves of a drink at my expense. In fact, that is a bit of a sore point because one of those members also scored a hole-in-one the following week and, as the news went round the course like wildfire, I looked forward to my drink at his expense. When I got into the bar, I found that he had purchased a bottle of whisky and left it on the bar, but it had all gone by the time I got to my turn! I went into the snooker room and said that I was looking for my drink and all he could say was that he had put a bottle behind the bar. I reminded him that I had specifically bought him a during the previous week, but he was unmoved, saying that it was my bad luck to get to the bar so late! One learns much about human behaviour in these circumstances.

One final point about that day – it was my girlfriend's birthday and she said that I would never forget my hole-in-one as it was her birthday, but the reality was that I never forgot her birthday as it was the day I scored my hole-in-one!

Back to my marshalling experiences. Having secured accommodation, I made my way north to join the team of marshals at the Great North Open (everything in the north seemed to be 'Great'!), where I was to meet quite a different group of marshals, but the operation was still organised by Barry and Mavis Drew.

I first got to know Ivor Robson, the official starter, at the beautiful course by the name of Slaley Hall. Again, I had arrived early and was on the course when Ivor appeared with his various bits and pieces to set up his stand by the first tee. I took the opportunity to ask him if I could take his photograph, explaining to him that I was collecting photographs of all the golfing greats that I met as a marshal.

"Och, why do ye want to bother with the likes of me?!" he asked in his lovely Scottish brogue, wondering why I would want to add him to my collection. He was a genial Scotsman who, with his full head of silvery-grey hair and distinctive bright green jacket, had become a regular feature of the major golf tournaments on the European Tour.

Ivor Robson – official photograph

Ivor Robson's autograph

I'd seen him countless times on television. He had introduced almost every known golfer for the previous twenty years – all done with his trademark announcement: "On the tee, from [place] and [name]" which would be spoken in his perfect pronunciation, no matter how complicated the Asian players' names. He took the trouble to check with the players beforehand as to how their names were pronounced – that was the measure of the man, meticulous planning were his watchwords.

I loved the way he had a quiet word with the players before making his announcement to the public. He would say, "Two minutes to go, gentlemen." Just before making the announcement, he would say – "Play well," and with that his eyes were firmly fixed on the large Rolex clock opposite. Ivor was a very precise man and no matter who was standing on the tee itching to drive off when the fairway in front was clear, he ensured that the play started precisely at twelve-minute intervals or whatever the allocated tee-off times dictated. I've seen Tiger Woods pacing back and forth while awaiting Ivor's announcement.

I read that Ivor had effectively tumbled into the job when he'd joined a company in 1975 and, on his first day, they sent him to The Open Championship at Carnoustie to act as announcer on the first tee. Having been a professional golfer before he decided to hang up his boots; he was now announcing golfers that he had previously played with shortly before. Apparently, after his first appearance, the R&A were so impressed with his performance that they asked his company if he could be the permanent announcer. His career lasted forty years, with his last job being The Open Championship in 2015 at St Andrews as befitted this great man. Indeed, the R&A presented him with a replica of The Claret Jug which was an honour normally attributed only to winners of the great trophy. He so deserved such an award for his contribution over the years and I count it as a real privilege to have known him.

Ivor was a true gentleman, as I found out in my many meetings with him after that first encounter. His constitution was legendary as he stood by the first tee from the first group to the last without any more than a brief five-minute break, if that. I recall asking him once how he managed to last that long without having to take a toilet break – indeed, I asked if he had a 'wee tube' threaded down inside his trouser leg and into some subterranean chamber. He had a chuckle at the absurdity of that suggestion but said he'd heard it many times before. He explained that he didn't drink more than a sip of water in the morning before heading to his station by the first tee. "And I may have a few dry biscuits as well!" His phrase was "Less input, less output!"

I was chatting to Ivor one morning and I noticed how his lectern was set out with various bits and pieces – a real Aladdin's Cave. To one side, a pile of A4 sheets showed the positions of the pins on the greens that day along with positions for the following day as well. Walking Scorers had been given a similar sheet but the information we had was about where to stand at each tee and green to allow for the best view and the quickest exit. He kept a box of long wooden tees, and I was always fascinated by how many of these would be grabbed by players and caddies alike. He often needed to have an umbrella to hand for unexpected rain showers and, in the hotter weather, he had a huge sunshade erected to protect him from the heat as he always wore the distinctive green jacket. In fact, I never saw Ivor in anything other than his 'Sunday best', as we used to call it, with his hair immaculately combed with just a hint of Brylcreem. At The Ryder Cup Matches, he swapped his distinctive green jacket for a smart blazer.

It is a mark of the man that, when I contacted him to tell him that I was writing a book that contained sections about him and I wanted his approval, he said that I must write what I want as it would be more interesting that way. I'll await his comments after he has read the book!

Working at Slaley Hall, I bumped into a couple of lovely ladies from time to time around the course and, on enquiring where they were from, one of them was Ian Garbutt's mum, Alice, who was accompanied by her friend, Pat. I would see them from time to time on various golf courses as they supported Ian when he played in the European Tour events. It was great to build such friendships while working as a volunteer.

The atmosphere around the course at The Great North Open seemed to be more relaxed than the golf courses in the Midlands and the players seemed to be more accessible, none more so than a personable young player called Andy Beal. I was talking to his caddie one morning and discreetly enquired why Andy always wore shades. Much to my embarrassment, I was told that Andy had been diagnosed with cancer a few years before and had had to have one eye removed. There, if ever I needed it, was a shining example of determination to overcome adversity. On reading about Andy afterwards, I discovered that he had finished third at

The Benson & Hedges Open in 1998. I also learned that he had had a special ball designed with red hexagons to aid his putting – the colour red after his beloved Southampton Football Club!

Nick Dougherty

I also bumped into Nick Dougherty with his caddie, Damon, on several occasions and marvelled at their cheery dispositions – they were always smiling. I see that Nick has now carved out a wonderful career for himself as a presenter of golf at the major tournaments and his open personality is very much suited to that role. I subsequently came across Damon on several occasions at different golf events, the most memorable being at the Forest of Arden when he was on José Maria Olazábal's bag. I was relaxing while watching play from the 18th tee when José Maria and Damon walked past. Ever the gentleman, Damon raised a hand in greeting, although judging by the look on his face, his golfer wasn't doing too well at that point, and it was inappropriate to stop for a chat.

Another real gentleman caddie was Colin Byrne, on the bag for Retief Goosen when I first met him at Slayley Hall. He always remembered me thereafter and the last time I saw him was at Carnoustie in 2018, where he was caddying for Ernie Els. He combined his caddying skills with that of a journalist and wrote for the *Irish Times*. Caddies are often a much-maligned group of people, but their hard work has underpinned many famous golfers and their ultimate success. At his peak, Steve Williams, Tiger Woods' caddie, was allegedly earning more than any other New Zealand sportsperson, including the golfer Michael Campbell.

Arriving early at golf courses as I did regularly, I would often come across caddies out with their notebooks to take special note of pin positions or any subtle changes on the course. At St Andrews one morning, I encountered Fanny Sunesson, one-time caddy for Nick Faldo, when she was out on the course on one such mission. She obligingly posed for a photograph which she later signed for me, and she always acknowledged me wherever we met. Last time I saw Fanny was while walking out on a training session at Royal Portrush in 2019 where she instantly recognised me, and we chatted as we walked. A lovely woman and an accomplished player at amateur level as well.

Fanny Sunesson   **Henrik Stenson and Fanny**

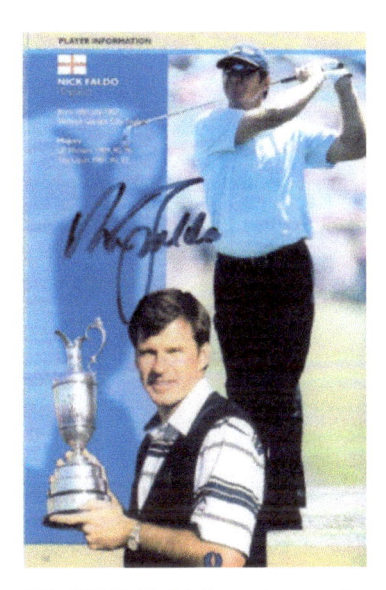

Sir Nick Faldo's autograph

While she was caddying for Henrik Stenson, I recall her patience with a group of young children who were shouting for Henrik to sign their autograph books. Fanny crouched down by the group and explained that Henrik needed to concentrate on his putting technique, but he would definitely spend some time with them when he had completed his routine. Surely enough, Henrik, to his eternal credit, came over and spent about half an hour with these children who were absolutely blown away by his charming personality. It just didn't fit with his image as 'The Ice Man' but it showed his love of the game and the need to encourage enthusiasm at all ages. I think that many top players could learn from Henrick's attitude in this respect as children are our future. I have found Phil Mickelson to be very similar in being free with his time for youngsters.

It is worth mentioning at this point the logistical challenge of formulating my unique collection of photographs whereby each photo was taken by me and then printed off for signature by the player at some future event. Having the right photograph at the right time became quite an art and I would sort the available photographs into the order in which the players were to be on the course. Naturally, it didn't always work out that I was able to ask the player for their signature and Todd Hamilton once asked me if I minded waiting while he finished his sandwich! I'd love to say that happened at Sandwich, but it was by the first tee at St Andrews.

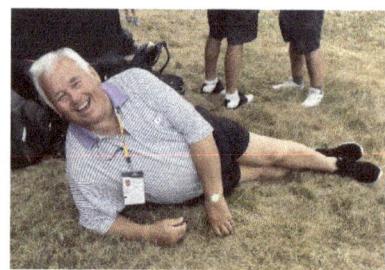

Todd Hamilton

**Keith Woodford –
ace autograph hunter!**

I have encountered several serious autograph hunters over the years but none so proficient as Keith Woodford and his friends. I really cannot remember where or when I first saw Keith's friendly face in the crowd, but I got to know him well. He had a fantastic collection of autographs and had the ability to get close to the players that he really wanted to add to his collection. The one photograph that fascinated me most was a glorious photograph of St Andrews where he had managed to obtain the signatures of all the living winners of The Open Championship. I was with him on a practice day at Carnoustie in 2018 when he showed me the document and, at that stage, he only required a signature from Jordan Spieth. I told him he'd better get a move on as Jordan was approaching our location. Keith and his friends asked me if I would guard their bags etc., while they headed off to approach Jordan between green and tee, where players were always happy to be stopped for autographs and photographs. Keith returned a few minutes afterwards proudly holding the signed photograph in his protective plastic wallet. I don't think that Keith was in it for the money but I'm sure that his collection of signatures would be worth a great deal on the open market.

Keith's collection of Open Winners' Autographs

Keith would pop up all over the place and, on my way to Royal Liverpool in 2006, I had just parked my car in the middle of a huge car park when a familiar voice behind me boomed out: "Dougie!" We walked to the course together; time with Keith was always valuable and he outlined his strategy for obtaining significant autographs that day. In all the time I've known Keith, I've never once abused his friendship by getting him to obtain a signature on one of my photographs and neither did he ask me to use my security pass status to get to players that were on his 'hit list'.

However, we did communicate with each other before tournaments when I would be seeking leads to find accommodation. Once or twice, I booked into a B&B that Keith and his friends had organised but, as usual, my problem was finding out that I hadn't been selected for that event. On one occasion, I had already paid a significant deposit – it was when The Open was held at Royal Birkdale – only to find that I had been unlucky and wasn't selected. I lost quite a bit of money, but 'a deal was a deal' and I knew that I was taking a risk. Keith managed to find someone to fill the void and I really didn't mind paying out.

At The English Open that year, I recall watching players teeing off in the Pro-Am, which was held on the Wednesday before the main event. The first four-ball was a group starring Michael Campbell from New Zealand, Bobby Davro – the TV personality and comedian – with two high handicap players. Michael Campbell drove off from the Championship tee, which seemed to be a long way back from where the others teed off. As the others approached the front tee, I did wonder about the sense of spectators standing right behind the ropes on either side of the fairway, effectively forming a tunnel of humanity between which the three remaining players would hit their shots. Bobby Davro stood on the tee, and observing the relative closeness of the crowd, he waved for the spectators to move back. On his command, people gradually edged back until they formed a V-shape.

Bobby held his hand up and said, "OK – that's fine!" and then hit a perfect drive right down the middle of the fairway! Unknown to me, he was an 11-handicap player and was just ensuring that the other two players wouldn't be inhibited by the proximity of the crowd when they were hitting their shots. I know that no one should stand anywhere that close when I was teeing off! I was always amazed that spectators would line the course while high handicap players hit their shots.

Later that year, when I read the Ryder Cup application form in detail, the enormity of the occasion hit me as there was a note pointing out that Monday 24th September was reserved for overseas volunteers, and UK residents were requested to attend the registration sessions on the Saturday or Sunday. The international aspect of the event really dawned on me. Part of the application form invited us to list the days that we were available and, anticipating the thrill of it all, I put my name down for every single day. No point holding back at this stage and showing willingness surely would be seen as a positive signal from me. In fact, I added a note: "I will be available for the whole week and will be happy to do whatever you want, whenever you want me to do it." I was determined to make a mark and that seemed to be a good way to get noticed at this early stage.

I was thrilled to receive the formal letter with the Ryder Cup logo in the top right-hand corner, confirming that I would be working "on scoring duties under the direction of John Wardle, Senior Marshal (Scoring) and his deputy, Peter Houghton". It was exactly what I had hoped to hear but, until that moment, I couldn't be certain that I would be in John's team. The list of benefits was interesting: "Coffee and Danish pastries will be supplied on arrival and cold drinks will be supplied during the day; a uniform will be supplied **free of charge** (in bold) comprising a waterproof top, 2 shirts, sleeveless sweater and hat all bearing the Ryder Cup logo; a 10% discount will be allowed against any purchases from the Official Merchandising and, finally, Ryder Cup Limited will be arranging an 'End of Match' party for all marshals."

So, the perks were substantial, together with an option to buy an entry ticket at face value for a friend or relative (given the popularity of the event, this was like gold dust).

September 2001 was written large in my diary as I was building up to the excitement of scoring at The Ryder Cup for the very first time. I visited The Belfry towards the end of August and I was really impressed with the infrastructure that was already in place, particularly a large leader board behind the iconic pond by the 18th green. It is truly remarkable how a golf course can be transformed with all the trappings of a major tournament and already the course had that aura of anticipation.

Doug by main logo on first tee

The Ryder Cup Matches, for those who may not be too familiar with the history, is a biennial men's golf competition between teams from Europe and the United States, which started way back in 1927 and is named after the English businessman, Samuel Ryder, who donated the now famous trophy. However, the first matches were played between Great Britain and the USA, but the dominance of the USA teams led to the inclusion of continental European golfers, prompted by the success of Spanish golfer Seve Ballesteros and other Spanish golfers. The event is jointly administered by the PGA of America and Ryder Cup Europe, so many of the top players in the world are involved. The success of the Ryder Cup Matches has led to a television audience of approximately one billion viewers in addition to the forty or fifty thousand spectators who are lucky enough to secure tickets each match day.

The format of the Matches:
Day 1 (Friday)   4 Fourball (better ball) matches in the morning.
4 Foursome (alternate shot) matches in the afternoon.
Day 2 (Saturday) 4 Fourball (better ball) matches in the morning.
4 Foursome (alternate shot) matches in the afternoon.
Day 3 (Sunday) 12 Singles matches.

The European Team consisted of **Darren Clarke, Padraig Harrington, Thomas Bjorn, Colin Montgomerie,** Pierre Fulke, **Lee Westwood, Paul McGinley**, Niclas Fasth, **Benhard Langer, Phillip Price**, Sergio Garcia and Jesper Parnevik. Their Captain was **Sam Torrance**. I had already seen and met the players in **bold,** but the others were going to be a whole new experience.

By contrast, I hadn't met or seen any of Team USA, which consisted of Tiger Woods, Phil Mickelson, David Duval, Mark Calcavecchia, David Toms, Davis Love lll, Scott Hoch, Jim Furyk, Hal Sutton, Stewart Cink, Scott Verplank, and Paul Azinger. Their Captain was Curtis Strange. This would be my first experience of the world's finest golfers playing right in front of me and it was hard to contain my excitement.

Another factor about the Ryder Cup is that these top players, almost to a man, would say that teeing off at the first hole induced a numbness in their bodies which sometimes resulted in their being happy just to hit the ball. In a pre-match interview, Sam Torrance famously said that "trying to explain what it's like to play in the Ryder Cup is a bit like trying to explain to a childless person what it's like to have a child". Sage words indeed.

Whilst I had been a fan of the Ryder Cup Matches as a television spectator, with vivid memories of Tony Jacklin etched in my mind, I couldn't really comprehend the sensation of being 'inside the ropes' at such a prestigious event attended by some of the most fervent supporters of any sport. It was a vision that both made my pulse race as well as an amazing feeling of apprehension as I would literally be rubbing shoulders with golfers from the world stage, something that I had hitherto not experienced.

In the month beforehand, I paid a visit to Scotland to see my family and attend a party to celebrate my younger twin brothers' 50th birthday on 10th September, which ran on after midnight, to my older brother's 60th birthday on 11th September. *Great planning*, I thought to myself and wondered how my parents had conjured up such a special occasion! The reverie was shattered as I travelled home to Bristol and one of my brothers rang me to find out if I had arrived home safely. When I answered that I was a few miles away, my brother told me to switch on my television as soon as I got home because I wouldn't believe what I would see. Sure enough, the images of those planes flying into the World Trade Centre in New York are indelibly etched in my brain.

Thoughts of the Ryder Cup Matches were far from the forefront of my mind, but the golfing press started to speculate about the possibility of the postponement of the event in view of the USA being in mourning for the lost lives. There was a school of thought that the Americans had prepared for the event and there was no better way of saluting the fallen than proceeding with the Ryder Cup Matches, particularly as the chosen teams had been selected on current form apart from anything else.

A statement was released: "The PGA of America has informed the European Ryder Cup Board that the scope of the last Tuesday's tragedy is so overwhelming that it would not be possible for the United States Ryder Cup Team and officials to attend the match this month."

As soon as it was known that the event was to be postponed for a year, The Chief Marshal had many requests from volunteers who wanted to buy the uniforms that had been produced for the 2001 date, but he confirmed that Ryder Cup Limited had declared that the existing supply would be put into storage and used the following year.

Of course, as history has confirmed, the event was postponed until 2002 and the tradition of the cup being played on odd-numbered years was broken for all time (or so I thought until a thing called a pandemic struck in 2020). The captains agreed that the same players would be selected to play twelve months later. Given that players were often chosen as wild cards because their current form put them in the picture for selection, it was to add another uncertain element to an already unique situation.

Due to the delay in playing the matches, the world rankings changed during the intervening twelve months, and it was interesting to note that, in Team Europe, only Niclas Fasth (33–32) and Sergio Garcia (7–5) had improved their positions. Note: the numbers in brackets show first the world rankings in 2001 and second the world ranking in 2002. Padraig Harrington had slipped from 12th to 79th, Lee Westwood from 20th to 148th and Phillip Price from 51st to 119th. In Team USA, the most significant changes in world rankings were David Duval from 3rd to 12th, Mark Calcavecchia from 18th to 42nd and Hal Sutton from 27th to 125th. Twelve months is a long time in golf!

Having visited The Belfry for some training sessions and seeing the massive infrastructure that had been set up to host the event, one can only marvel at the reorganisation that had to be implemented to delay the competition by twelve months. The phrase: "It's an ill wind that blows no good" must have resonated with lucky golfers who played The

Brabazon Course at The Belfry in the intervening twelve months, as they would be able to imagine playing in front of the crowds with all the grandstands still in position.

Team Europe fans   **Team USA fans**

Doug with some Team USA fans

I had played the Brabazon course in 1999 with two friends when I celebrated my fiftieth birthday, so I was familiar with the topography and subtleties of the various holes, particularly the famous tenth hole – a Par 4 – where Seve drove the green on his way to a courageous eagle in 1989. When I played the hole, I sensibly laid up short of the pond for safety, and promptly hit my second shot into the stream just in front of the well-protected green. Mind you, I probably visited parts of that course that The Ryder Cup players were unlikely ever to see! Sadly, Pete Clews and Andy Murdoch are no longer with us both having passed away since the photographs below were taken. We were members at Gaudet Luce Golf Club in Droitwich Spa and played regularly on Sunday mornings where each hole was fought for as if we were playing at The Open Championship. The magnificent sum of ten pence per hole was the wager in those days!

Pete Clews and Andy Murdoch celebrating Doug's 50th birthday at The Belfry in 1999

**"Doug celebrating his 50th birthday at
The Belfry in 1999".**

It is interesting to note that, when I moved from Llantwit Major where I was a member at Southerndown Golf Club to Droitwich Spa in 1992, I applied to join Droitwich Golf Club and I had to attend an interview before a panel of three club members, including the Captain and Club Secretary. I was told that I had to wait for eighteen months before I could join due to the fact that there was a waiting list. I was staggered at this comment because it meant that I couldn't continue playing the sport I loved. No doubt, there wouldn't have been a problem if I had been a low handicap player and able to play for one of their teams! In order to continue playing, I joined a brand-new club called Gaudet Luce and never regretted that decision as I met some wonderful people there and was able to observe a new course mature into the lovely club it is nowadays.

By contrast, when I moved from Clevedon to Thornbury in 2018, I applied to join Thornbury Golf Centre and was given a case of wine together with some other inducements. Golf had become so popular that many golf clubs were advertising for new members. In 2020, the situation showed signs that the golf bubble had burst whereby I took photographs of the North Worcestershire Golf Club (where I had played several times) which had been sold off as housing development land. As a keen golfer, I was saddened to see that the course had grown over although the outlines of many holes were still visible as can be seen in the image below.

The builders move in   **Housing development on former golf course in Worcester**

Returning to 2002, the Ryder Cup Matches eventually went ahead in September, the pre-match excitement was heightened by the world of golf looking at this as an opportunity to forget 'The Battle of Brookline' in 1999 where, it must be said, golf standards dropped with that infamous invasion of the 17th green after Justin Leonard holed an enormous putt, but José Maria Olazábal still had the possibility of sinking his putt. The USA team and their wives ran on to the putting surface in an unbridled showing of jubilation – an occurrence that was to reverberate around the world of golf.

Alistair Cooke, in his 'Letter from America', described the last day of that tournament as "a date that will live in infamy".

Both Captains were keen to ensure that those scenes were never to be repeated but, of course, it only served to raise the volume in an event that was already full of passion, tension, and desire. Curtis Strange – Captain of Team USA

- in his speech at the Opening Ceremony, and Sam Torrance – Captain of Team Europe - both predicted that the Ryder Cup Matches would be played in the true spirit of the game, and it was everyone's responsibility to ensure that it happened that way. Indeed, in a television interview with both Sam and Curtis, they acknowledged that Brookline was not the best day for golf, and they needed to make an apology and move on. Their words were heeded, and the event was to be a glorious advertisement for all that is best in the competitive sport of golf at the highest level.

The security for The Ryder Cup Matches – following on so soon after the atrocities of the Twin Towers in New York – was stepped up to an airport-type security with bag searches and body scanners. Given that forty thousand spectators would pass through this system, it proved to be an immense task. This was set up at the nearby NEC (National Exhibition centre) where there was ample car parking, and a bus transfer system was set up to take everyone to The Belfry in a controlled manner. I heard that one spectator had managed to smuggle his mobile phone on to the course inside his shoe! As we were part of the volunteer group, we went through security before the public and then we were transported to The Belfry in minibuses. Talking to one or two spectators later, I appreciated how fortunate we were to be spared the lengthy queues that formed as spectators arrived in their thousands.

The bus journey to The Belfry was one of mounting excitement as marshals started chatting and discussing their previous experiences at such events. For me, that was part of the excitement as it dawned on me that I really was going to be there and part of something special. Cameras were allowed on the practice days – it was before the advent of the mobile phone as a camera – and I managed somehow to leave my camera in the Scorers' Headquarters overnight, so I had it in my pocket for all three days of the competition. I can be the master of discretion and I was to ensure that it didn't come out until after the golf had been played when no one seemed at all interested about who was filming what!

On the course itself, security was ever-present and never more so than when I saw the police with their sniffer dogs complete close inspections for the grandstands. The reality of the need for tight security was right there. However, the most memorable sight on the golf course in the early hours was the teams of groundsmen, in their giant-sized mowing machines, crosscutting the immaculate fairways that were still covered in dew before the sun rose, their little headlights weaving a fantastic pattern like a coordinated display by fireflies. The hard work that goes into preparing a championship course is mostly done out of the public gaze.

It was an incredibly smoothly run operation and, on Day 1, which was the Opening Ceremony, the Walking Scorers were directed to a personal briefing by the Tournament Director – it was at that point that I realised what an important and privileged role I would be playing. There were only fifteen of us, together with John Wardle and Pete Houghton. Out of the hundreds of volunteers at the course, I was one of a very select group and proud to be included as a 'rookie' volunteer scorer. We had a briefing that would emphasise the importance of our work and an appreciation of what we were about to do.

Scoring Marshals prepare for their briefing

One of the other Walking Scorers came up to me after the briefing and asked if I had a son living in Swansea. This was Leighton and I found that he knew my son, Chris, very well. Leighton was a lovely young man, and I always enjoyed his company both at the Ryder Cup and The Wales Open, which was more his territory. This exemplifies one of the real pleasures in volunteering – the making of new and lasting friendships.

Firstly, we were briefed on the protocol – "No chatting to players or caddies" – which was standard for volunteer scorers. Also, no showing bias, as we were to remain neutral throughout the event. As things progressed, and looking back later at TV coverage, I noticed that this factor was quickly forgotten by many volunteers when the matches drew to their conclusions!

At the end of the briefing, we were each handed a card with our duties indicated for each of the three competition days.

My card showed:

Tuesday: Practice – General marshalling under the guidance of Graham Faulkner.
Wednesday: Practice – Reserve.
Thursday: Training AM and Opening Ceremony PM.
Friday: AM Match No.3 – PM – Reserve.
Saturday: AM – Leader board 3 – PM – Reserve.
Sunday: Match No.12

When I read the card, I immediately looked at my duties for the final day and, as it was the final match, I immediately thought that it may be the decider and the whole competition would rest on that result or, more likely, it may just be a 'dead rubber' – in other words a match of little consequence as the Ryder Cup would probably have been decided by then. How wrong could I be? Of course, the final day's singles match pairings were not declared until the Saturday evening after the play had finished on the day. Spectators and journalists alike were keen to see the pairings as soon as they were announced by the captains of the USA and European Teams respectively.

What John Wardle hadn't mentioned was that the scoring system would be totally different and would involve walking with the players. I hadn't experienced that before but was certainly looking forward to inclusion in such a small group. In addition, handheld computers would be used so that every shot could be recorded in 'real time'. Also, the scoring information was going to be relayed to the world of golf and beyond, to an audience that was only exceeded by the Olympic Games and the football World Cup. Probably just as well that John didn't mention these facts as it would have been the best-known laxative to man if he had! However, the apprehension was eased when, after a hands-on training session with the handheld computer devices, we were allowed out on the course to test the equipment live. It was wonderful opportunity to see these top golfers practising in a relaxed mood before the heat of battle at the weekend.

I managed to follow Colin Montgomerie for a few holes and, although I didn't witness it myself, he famously handed his golf club to a wag in the crowd who had berated him for playing some indifferent shots around the green. Apparently, having heard this chap go on and on, Colin finally walked over to him and handed him his club and said something like, "If you're so good, have a go!" Much to everyone's amusement, this chap chipped the ball to within a foot of the pin and Colin retrieved his club before walking on shaking his head. Colin really was the talisman of the European Team, and it was great to see how relaxed he was with the spectators. He got some bad press in the USA, but I have to say that he was always gracious whenever I asked him for a photograph or autograph.

I should point out here that, as volunteers, we were allowed an additional pass for a friend or colleague to visit the Ryder Cup Matches and I gave my pass to a former colleague with whom I had worked in Birmingham. He arranged to come to the course on the Wednesday as he wanted to see Tiger Woods in the flesh and that was one of the official practice days where I had on-course marshalling duties 'inside the ropes'.

However, Tiger was to prove elusive in that he went on the course to practise with his good friend Mark Calcavecchia, and they set off at 5:30am, returning at 7:30am. I walked with them for several holes along with about eight or nine other marshals who wanted to watch the great man practise in relative tranquillity with no spectators around. I learned that these two were good friends and often practised together. It was quite something to be standing on the tee with Tiger Woods and observing his long drives, something that I'll never forget. They finished their session at about 7am and headed back to the clubhouse and I never imagined for a moment that they wouldn't reappear later when the public were allowed in. With the gates opening at 8am, this meant that no spectators saw Tiger Woods practising that day. He seemed to show an unwillingness to partake in the team spirit of the event and many spectators were disappointed because they had come to watch the practice sessions specifically to see him. As I was on general marshalling duties that day, the question I was asked mostly was "Where is Tiger?" to which I could only say that I didn't know but he might be out again soon.

It was somewhat embarrassing to meet up with my friend, who had brought his young son along for the pleasure of seeing Tiger Woods and ended up with a 'no show' by The Tiger.

When the event got underway on the Friday, I hadn't realised how many people would be walking around with each match and I often had to move smartly to get ahead of the following herd around the greens. All the players' wives and girlfriends were equipped with special Ryder Cup flat cushions for kneeling on the wet grass. I even exchanged a few pleasantries with Sam Torrance, who always wears his heart on his sleeve – a charming gentleman. Etched on his face was the determination and commitment to the task; having once sunk the winning putt at this very venue in 1985 when Europe's win ended twenty-eight years of American domination, he clearly wanted to experience that same thrill as captain.

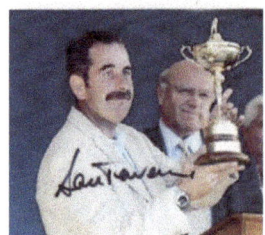

**Autographs of Monty, Sam Torrance,
John Wilkie and Paul McGinley**

It is worth mentioning John Wilkie here. He was Sam Torrance's caddie and I had seen him around a couple of the events that I had already attended as a volunteer. He was a most jovial and hardworking man. He worked non-stop in the run up to the Opening Ceremony and I was mightily impressed by his work ethic. He supported Sam admirably in this magnificent team effort. John even signed a photograph for me afterwards and I treasure that as much as those of some of the top professionals.

Day 1 – Friday – Team Europe won the first three four-ball matches, and I was Walking Scorer with Match No.3: Colin Montgomerie & Bernhard Langer v Scott Hoch and Jim Furyk. The European pairing was an interesting choice by Sam Torrance as 'Monty' had frequently shown his disdain for Langer's slow, meticulous play whereas he liked 'to get on with it'. Nevertheless, it turned out to be an inspired selection as they won their match with a convincing 4&3 score line to put more blue on the leader boards with Europe leading by 3-1 at the end of the morning session. The afternoon matches saw Team USA claw their way back into contention as only Garcia & Westwood gained a point for Team Europe. The overnight score was 5½-3½.

In Match No.3, the Match Referee was a Welshman who just asked to be called DJ – I didn't enquire further – and he was a gem, giving me clear instructions about what he expected of me throughout the round. I learned a great deal from him, particularly where to position myself for the best view of play without getting in the line of the players, the television cameras and, most importantly, not blocking out the view of any spectators who had all paid substantially to be there. I was to meet DJ again when I worked at The Open Championship; he was always the gentleman and greeted me as an old friend.

When we reached the now famous 10th Hole – a Par 4 which Seve had famously driven in the Ryder Cup Matches in 1989 (and made eagle) – I was taking my position to the right of the players on the tee when a voice from the crowd said, "Doug Fowler! What the hell are you doing there?!"

The voice was that of Russ Lewis (see earlier photograph), an architect that I had worked with in Cardiff back in 1986 when he was still a student. We had played golf together all that time ago. He was truly taken aback to see me 'inside the ropes' as we had lost touch and he had no idea that I was an active Walking Scorer at such events. I think his friends were impressed that he knew an official who was involved in the tournament

The golf was of the highest quality, and I got a close-up view of Jim Furyk's unique golf swing! However awkward it looked; it was very effective with Jim hitting some of the best iron shots I have ever seen. At one point, he hit his drive close to the water's edge on a long Par 5 hole and he had to take off his shoes and socks to stand in the water before he could take his second shot. I'd seen film of players having to do that when I had watched golf on the TV but never had I seen it 'in the flesh'. To his eternal credit, he hit a remarkable shot on to the green. Of course, I had to remind myself that these were the top players in the world and such brilliance was to be expected.

On the day, Colin and Bernhard were 'hot', hitting long irons close to the pin on several holes and eventually winning 4 & 3. I've never seen such a display of long iron play from both sides, and I marvelled at their ability to hit the green from two hundred yards or more. It was a masterclass in approach play with the Europeans prevailing in the end.

Colin's putter was on form, and I recall being behind him when one of his putts snaked down the green and plopped into the hole to the sound of a resounding cheer from the European fans. I even had a 'high five' with his wife, Eimear, following which I looked around to ensure that I wasn't seen by other officials as I had temporarily forgotten our duty to be neutral! The emotion of the moment was hard to keep in especially when the American fans were shouting their support so loudly.

Day 2 – Saturday – my job was to operate a leader board out on the course and, while I missed the intensity of walking with play, I managed to see more golf as all matches passed our way. That was when I noticed how well-planned the golf course was in that huge groups of spectators could follow certain matches around, such was the layout and topography of The Belfry. By the end of play, Team USA had evened the score line with wins by Michelson & Toms, Woods & Love lll, Calcavecchia & Duval, then again by Woods & Duval. The score level at 8-8 at the end of the day and all to play for on Sunday.

On the Saturday evening, I eagerly awaited the posting of the pairings for the singles on Sunday. Sam Torrance's strategy was to get his top players out first so that the leader board filled up with blue and would give the lower order matches inspiration. Curtis Strange did exactly the opposite with the result, so that the final pairing was Tiger Woods v Jesper Parnevik! Imagine my reaction on reading that. This was to be my scoring match the following day.

I thought, *this is going to be fantastic – in the company of Tiger Woods for 18 holes! My mates will be so jealous.* Once it sunk in, I also realised that there would be incredible pressure on me with the 'circus' of press and vociferous fans that usually follows Tiger around any golf course.

Walking alongside Tiger, I realised the pressure on him from his supporters who called out to him at all parts of the course. Some American supporters would shout things like, "Tiger, I love you!" It's no wonder that Tiger was in a 'bubble' with his caddie, Steve Williams, throughout the match and I had no eye contact with him for the entire eighteen holes. Our group even had the accompaniment of a few police officers, such was the security around this man. I had read that he would be 'in the zone' when out on the golf course and this, to be fair, wasn't a surprise as he needed total concentration to retain the position of World No.1.

Jesper, by contrast, was an affable player and frequently wandered alongside me to enquire how some of the other matches were going; he had spotted how I was receiving updates in my earpiece from my radio. He was altogether more of a 'team' player, showing a great interest in how the competition was going elsewhere on the course. At least that was how it seemed to me.

Jesper Parnevik **My Scorer's armband signed by Colin Montgomerie and others**

The Match Referee was Mike Stewart, a friendly official whom I was to meet from time to time at The Open where he was a European Tour Rules Official. I marvelled at his understanding of the complexities of the Rules of Golf, which many club golfers view as the 'dark art'.

Day 3 – Sunday – Team Europe Captain Sam Torrance's strategy was to prove indeed inspired as Team Europe went on to win the Ryder Cup by a score of 15½ to 12½ with, perhaps, the most significant win being Phillip Price vanquishing Phil Michelson – World No.119 beating World No.2! When interviewed afterwards, Phillip famously said that he'd told Lee Westwood earlier to, "Tell them who I beat!" It was certainly the talk around the course at the next Wales Open.

As it happened, Match No.12 did work out to be a 'dead rubber' as Paul McGinley sank the winning putt on the 18th green while our match was still on the 15th hole. The sounds around the course were deafening and it was hard to concentrate knowing that Team Europe had already won a handsome victory. As it was, Tiger decided to battle on until the completion of his game, which ended on the 18th green in a halved match. I know some critics said that he ought to have conceded a halved match to allow the celebrations to begin but Tiger just wanted to complete his match. I think that, as his record in singles wasn't that great, he just wanted to prove a point, but it didn't work out that way.

Europe won the Ryder Cup by a margin of 15½ to 12½ – the largest win since 1985. Indeed, at one point in the day, Europe had accumulated four and a half points from a possible six – exactly what Sam wanted, with the leader boards showing a large chunk of blue early in the day.

Celebrations had been put on hold, out of respect for Tiger and Jesper as we made our way up the 18th fairway, although I have to say that journey on foot was one of the scariest I have experienced as the spectators pushed in behind us as we approached the pond in front of the green. Indeed, we had to get a move on to avoid the weight of the spectators from forcing us into the water! Police and marshals were unable to restrain a crowd of about ten thousand on the fairway and we made our way through by the skin of our teeth.

However, the noise (as John Wardle had predicted) was deafening as we walked up to the green; I had never experienced anything like it before on any golf course. I can now imagine what it is like for sportsmen and women performing in front of huge crowds. After Jesper and Tiger agreed a half, we all shook hands on the green. I asked Tiger if he would autograph my scorer's armband, but he totally blanked me and walked straight off the green! Having walked for eighteen holes with him I thought he would oblige by signing; after all, I had my sharpie pen in my hand ready to give him. I think the occasion had gotten to him as he probably wanted to win his singles and he was undoubtedly disappointed that Team USA had lost.

Colin Montgomerie witnessed this 'snub' and kindly signed my armband instead. I also hugged Sam Torrance before leaving the green; he was in such a state with tears rolling down his cheeks. The scenes around the 18th green were some of the most memorable moments of my golfing experience, or indeed my life – unbelievable joy unbounded. Grown men were openly weeping with delight and fans were clamouring to share their congratulations with the players and their caddies. It was a struggle to make it through to our compound.

Match play can come down to who has the most desire, and sometimes luck, to prevail whereas Phillip Price's achievement was more of the former and less of the latter. Another notable fact was that it was Paul McGinley's halved match with Jim Furyk that clinched the win and his winning putt on the 18th hole is featured on most re-runs of any Ryder Cup Matches on television.

Following my match, I was still on the 18th green when Paul McGinley was 'helped' into the pond in front of the green along with an Irish flag to complete a scene that went viral around the world. It was probably the result of Darren Clarke's enthusiasm for his fellow countryman. Those scenes were of sheer jubilation and partying went on well into the night, including our own marshals' party at which I had to show restraint as I was driving home afterwards.

I was very proud to have been involved at such a high level in such a fabulous golf event and my dreams had really been fulfilled in that respect. Also, I had a cap, shirts, and jacket to wear with pride thereafter. It was always a joy to walk out on my local golf course with a branded jacket, cap, or shirt. I was frequently asked, when I had watched top-level golf played by the best players in the world, why it hadn't rubbed off on my own playing skills. Another aspect to my volunteering at the Ryder Cup Matches was the memory of Constantino Rocca once saying, "I may have helped win the Ryder Cup but, more important than that, I have made twelve new friends for life!"

I 'get' that and felt much the same way afterwards.

The European Ryder Cup Team 2004

**I have managed to obtain all the autographs of the
2004 Ryder Cup Team**

John and Peter congratulate each other on a job well done

A very tired young marshal!

This section would not be complete without mentioning Hilda Wardell (and her husband Roger who sadly passed away a few years ago), a disabled lady who attended all the golf tournaments at The Belfry, including the Ryder Cup Matches, where I first met her.

Hilda with Ian Woosnam OBE at The Belfry

Hilda and Roger with a group of marshals

Although I was a Walking Scorer for these matches, I was always aware of the plight of disabled spectators who often struggled to get a decent view of the golf. Indeed, some unreasonable marshals would often deny them access 'inside the ropes', where their view would be unimpeded, and they would be in no one's way. The Senior Marshal in that area was an unusually grumpy individual and he was muttering as I headed on my way. After all, what difference did it make if a wheelchair user was inside the ropes? They would hardly invade the green!

I can remember helping Hilda into a better viewing position and I immediately knew that this was a lovely lady with a wonderful spirit. Surely enough, we got on very well and she introduced me to her loving husband, Roger, who always attended the golf tournaments with her. Hilda told me of her love of golf and how she had met Seve Ballesteros, and had a photograph taken with him. It was her pride and joy.

I have an enduring memory of the time that I was 'off duty' but still wore my scorer's badge to allow me access to all areas of the course. I came across Hilda by the 10th green at The Belfry and we were having a chat when Ian Woosnam came walking nearby as he'd left the green during a practice round. Hilda told me that she was a great fan of 'Woosie', so with that, I called Ian over and asked if I could take a photograph of him with Hilda. He duly obliged and I managed to take a lovely photo which Ian later signed. I presented the signed photo to Hilda during my next visit to The Belfry. All in a day's work as a volunteer marshal and caring human being.

Hilda and I exchange Christmas cards and I keep in touch with her – she is a gem of a lady!

Shortly after the Ryder Cup had been presented to the European team, I was chatting to Padraig Harrington just outside the clubhouse. A bunch of TV men suddenly appeared, announcing that they were from the BBC and wanting to interview him, so I stepped aside, and the interview started. No sooner had Padraig started to talk about his singles match against Mark Calcavecchia – which he had won 5&4 – then a mobile phone rang out loud and clear.

The TV man cursed and said, "Who the hell hasn't switched off their phone?!"

Padraig casually reached into his back pocket, pulled out his phone and said, "Hi, Dad!" and started a conversation with his father, who had called from Ireland to congratulate him on his success.

I'll never forget the irritated look on the BBC man's face as he abandoned the interview!

Extracts from my folder including autographs from Padraig Harrington and Phillip Price

All in all, the Ryder Cup experience was all I hoped it would be and more. The excitement of the golf, the banter with the boisterous fans and the wonderment at the competitiveness of these top players were wonders to behold. The thing that seems to separate the Ryder Cup from the golfing majors, is the fist-pumping that goes on – an action not seen at other golf tournaments. A real privilege for someone who had only been involved in volunteering for such a relatively short period. My return journey home afterwards was filled with enough memories to write several books.

CHAPTER 5 (2003)
THE WALES OPEN & THE OPEN
(ROYAL ST GEORGE'S)

At Celtic Manor, where The Wales Open was held, scoring was quite a straightforward job during which each shot played was marked on an A5 paper scorecard as the round progressed. This was in addition to the scores that the players themselves kept on their own scorecards. Players' final scores could be ratified by them before the final score was published around the course and I sometimes asked players to sign my record after they had finished their round, just for my own interest. The scoring function, at that time, was to deal purely with scores on each hole – no information was required in terms of drive distances and the like. This was a basic system and, to be honest, would be of little use in the event of dispute where a player recorded an incorrect score for any hole after the round was completed. That never happened in my experience although I often worried about the need for my input in such a case.

Typical scorecard – signed by Darren Fichardt and Mark McNulty

In the absence of a Walking Referee, I would always check the scores with the caddies from time to time even though this wasn't always considered to be the best way to ensure accuracy. The caddies that I got to know would have been disappointed if anyone thought their information was less than accurate.

During the second round at The Wales Open, I was scoring for a three-ball that included an Australian player called Terry Price and, on the 3rd hole – a long Par 5 which had quite a drop in it – he carved his shot left with a massive hook. His ball hit a spectator on the head and St John's Ambulance were called to check him over. By the time we got down to that part of the course, the spectator had been buggied back to the base to receive attention. Marshals on the spot reported that he had said he felt OK, but the medics insisted on carrying out a complete check just in case.

When our group arrived at the Par 3 13th hole, I noticed the injured spectator standing in the crowd; he was easily identified by the white bandaging wrapped around his head with a little bloodstain on the forehead area. I pointed him out to Terry Price, who reached into his bag, pulled out a brand-new golf ball and signed it with his felt pen. He handed it to the injured spectator and apologised for his errant shot. When Terry came back to the tee area, I whispered to him, "If you'd hit me on the head with a golf ball, you'd be looking to pay significantly more in damages." I should have been careful what I said to him as he was an ex-boxer!

Ieuan Evans and Doug **Doug with Will Carling OBE**

Doug with supermodel Jodie Kidd

At The Wales Open, like many of the European Tour events where I volunteered as a marshal, there were lots of opportunities to meet celebrities on the Pro-Am days which were held on the Wednesdays before the tournament got underway on Thursdays. I have a fond memory of meeting the supermodel, Jodie Kidd, who was actually playing golf when she happily stopped for the photograph above. I managed to get the image printed and took it to the course the following day – "Ladies Day" – when she autographed the image for me much to the envy of my fellow volunteers. I also recall meeting Mark Williams – World Champion Snooker player – and commented on how laid back he was while playing golf. It was an attribute that earned him success at snooker, and he still competes at the highest level to this very day. Ieuan Evans – the Welsh rugby legend was a delight to walk with and he graciously recorded a message for my grandson, Ben, who was just getting started in his rugby playing career at the time. A lovely touch and a treasured memory.

On 13th June 2003, I received a final confirmation letter from the R&A Secretary, Michael Wells, that I had been selected to act as a scorer at The Open that year and my excitement levels rocketed as I read it.

The letter was final confirmation that I was going to be volunteering at The Open, which was being held at Royal St George's, Sandwich, in Kent. This was the 132nd Open Championship and I was going to be part of it. I had to read the letter several times and take in the enormity of being selected as a Scoreboard Operator/Carrier. The idea of walking around a golf course carrying a board didn't have as much appeal as working from the relative luxury of a scoreboard, but these fears were soon dispersed when I rang the R&A Office, and they confirmed that I had been allocated a job on the scoreboard by the 12th hole.

Excitement unbridled and I noted that scoreboard operators were paid £150.00 for the week whereas scoreboard carriers were to be paid £140.00. Somehow, I thought that those rates should be the other way round until I got there and understood the importance of the scoreboard operators being responsible for the accuracy of posting scores for the benefit of the paying public.

Michael's letter also enclosed details of where I was to attend for training and tickets for access to the course on the Sunday and Monday before my training session on the

Tuesday. I was thrilled at the thought of being able to watch world-class players practising and having an opportunity to walk the course before my duties began. I was rather amused by the warning that weather conditions could change so suitable wet or dry clothing should be worn.

Volunteers were to find their own accommodation and make their own travel arrangements to the course. I was so excited that I would have happily paid a fee for the privilege of working at such a prestigious event. Planning for accommodation, etc., was always provisional until confirmation of your selection was received from the R&A and, as this didn't come through until March or even as late as April, this made it quite difficult to make advanced bookings.

However, receiving the initial confirmation letter in January made finding accommodation quite easy. I checked out the Tourist Information and found a reasonably priced B&B on the outskirts of the town. The golfing community were given access to reasonably priced accommodation, and this was welcome as some local hotels would be charging exorbitant rates during the week of The Open.

I drove to Sandwich on the Sunday before the event and, on arrival, I was made to feel very much at home by a charming couple whose daughter had moved out of the family home quite recently. I was shown to my room and offered a meal although I had to make my excuses as I simply wanted to get to the golf course as soon as I could. My letter of acceptance had enclosed a temporary pass to the course, and I was keen to drink in the atmosphere there. Many golfers turn up at these events more than a week beforehand so that they can play the course and familiarise themselves with its idiosyncrasies. I wanted to experience that as well.

The deal was for bed and breakfast although I left their house at 5:30am and only had a coffee and toast before leaving in the morning. However, the wife insisted that I join them for dinner in the evening when I returned from the golf course. That was lovely and felt more like a home from home. I was even invited into their sitting room to watch television after dinner. I was usually fast asleep within a few minutes of sitting down after a tiring day walking the course.

The room that I had was just perfect. That is if you like frilly curtains and a whole room decorated in pale pink, just as their daughter had left it several years before. Nevertheless, it was exactly what I needed, with a small ensuite shower room.

One evening, while the husband was out at his bowls club, I had dinner alone with his wife and she confessed that her reason for renting out the room to me was that she wanted a new picture window in the kitchen. Her husband had told her that she had to rent out the room and take in some money if she wanted her new window so badly. The rate was so reasonable that I gave her a bonus of £100.00 before I left. She'd let it slip out that she was just short of the required total for the new window! Their hospitality had been excellent and made me feel very much part of their family.

This was my first stint at The Open Championship, and I was impressed with the organisation of the event. Not surprisingly, the R&A had honed their arrangements to a fine point after over a century of running the world's oldest golfing major. Their attention to detail was a revelation to me and their health and safety form – which all applicants had to complete with a declaration of our ability to do the job – was evidence that they took their responsibilities seriously, even down to listing any medications taken by applicants.

One phrase that stuck in my mind was the reference to *The Guide to Safety at Sports Grounds* (known as *The Green Guide*), which places a requirement on all event organisers to ensure that those appointed to act on their behalf meet certain criteria, including a requirement to be "fit and active with the maturity, character and temperament to carry out the duties required of them". I had already come to know several marshals to whom this didn't apply!

I confess to having been a little nervous when the form asked me to acknowledge that I would be undertaking duties that "may be physically demanding", as I had recurring knee problems. In fact, I was to visit my knee specialist, who would arrange for me to have a cortisone injection which worked wonders, rather like a squirt of WD40 to lubricate my right knee. Walking eighteen holes over links topography can be a gruelling experience for someone of my height and bulk. Thankfully, my first duties would be carried out inside a hut on the course and wouldn't involve too much walking.

When I first walked on to the course at Royal St George's in Sandwich, I had a sense of awe about the whole thing, which started with their glorious clubhouse. This location was the first that The Open Championship had been played at outside Scotland when it hosted the event in 1894 and more Open Championships have been hosted there than any other course outside Scotland. The place just reeked of history, and I confess to being absorbed by the ambience of the place.

At the training session on the Tuesday, I was given my access pass to the course, along with a parking pass and, most important of all, a couple of shirts, a waterproof jacket, and a baseball style cap. I have to say at this stage that the term 'waterproof' was a misnomer as I found out one day when it rained, and my 'showerproof' jacket leaked!

Nevertheless, it felt good to have our 'Unisys' shirts – that was the name of the company which was responsible for the scoring services. It was exciting to be part of such an important team of volunteers from all over the country and abroad. I sat next to a couple from California during the briefing and discovered that they had been volunteering and coming to The Open for more than ten years.

My duties were different to anything I had done at my previous tournaments, and I was allocated to be part of a small team that would run a leader board by hole 12. I was to be joined there by two teenage girls – Alice and Steffi, neither of whom were golfers, but they just volunteered for the fun of it – and Bobby, who was a young single-figure handicap golfer. Aged fifty-four, I was therefore the senior member of our team, but it was a meritocracy and worked exceedingly well. I didn't make anything of the fact that I was the only one who was given an armband with 'SCORER' in large letters on it!

The operation of a greenside leader board was quite a challenging task because, like all duties at The Open, everything understandably had to be precise and immediate. We were located directly opposite a public stand where spectators may be seated for hours on end and our board was the only source of scores information in that area. There were two boards on the front of our hut – the larger board was a mini version of the comprehensive leader boards that were situated around the course, displaying the top ten or twelve players at that moment. Alongside the large board, there was a smaller board known as the 'approach board', which displayed the current group on that hole together with the next group to arrive at the green.

Updated scores were radioed to us together with a handheld computer device that confirmed the same information. Armed with a printed start-time sheet, this made the operation simpler, and the thinking was that scoreboard operators would get ahead of the game by sorting out the groups of players in threes on the first two days of competition before the cut into neat piles on the floor below the drop-down hatches which allowed us to load the names from inside the hut. It would be a cardinal sin if the names displayed didn't correspond with the players currently on, or approaching, the green in question AND their current scores had to be accurately displayed. I have seen a board where the operators mistakenly managed to put the names in upside down! That didn't last for long as a sharp-eyed marshal nearby prompted them to sort it out quickly.

I realised then, ahead of my time, that the processing of such important information should be digitised and sent electronically rather than relying on the human intervention which could lead to mistakes. Indeed, at a later event – The Open at St Andrews in 2005 – I heard a newly appointed scorer had posted a hole-in-one on a par 5 hole thereby placing the player at the top of the leader board albeit for only the briefest of periods while the error was corrected, and the scorer was hastily replaced!

Thankfully, these huts at least had a roof which was to prove beneficial when the rain came. Alongside the hut, to the left, was a small platform on which we could stand and watch the action on the green; provided, of course, that our board was bang up to date. It was one of the perks of the job; a grandstand view of the top players putting out on the green below our 'grandstand' position.

A typical greenside leader board

At Royal St George's – Alice, Steffi, Doug & Bobby

The first two days of the tournament were quite straightforward because the groupings were published the evening beforehand and this made the sorting out of names quite simple whereas, after the cut, the pairings would change from the Saturday to the Sunday, hence the need for an efficient storage system in alphabetical order so that the names could be used then be replaced for the following day.

During the event, I was fascinated to note that most Walking Scorers were women and I wondered if there was an opportunity for men to perform that role. I decided that, in future, I would like to do that – walk with players – even with my knee replacement issue in the background of my mind.

On my first morning at the course, I turned up at 5:30 and headed straight for the putting green area as that was a good place to catch up with any golfers going about their practice routines. I spotted a lone golfer heading my way and to be honest I didn't recognise him. Nevertheless, I asked politely if I could take his photograph and he readily agreed. This was too good an opportunity to miss.

After taking the photo, feeling rather embarrassed, I said that I was not sure about his name, and he proudly replied, "My name is Ben Curtis and I'm from the US of A!" I later learned that he was born in Columbus Ohio and had arrived in Sandwich the week before so that he could have a good look at the course. He employed a local caddie – Andy Sutton – and they were a virgin duo for this most important championship.

This was Ben's first visit to The Open Championship, so I wished him good luck. He only went on to win it! He was leader in the clubhouse when Thomas Bjorn had his mishap at the 16th hole. If I had been a betting man, I would have taken good note that his odds were five hundred to one as he hadn't won a tournament anywhere before.

Ben Curtis – winner of The Open in 2003

Thomas Bjorn and Doug

Gary Player's autograph

Ben signed the photograph when I caught up with him at St Andrews in 2005. I was to follow his career thereafter but, unfortunately, it seemed that his win at Sandwich was a 'one hit wonder'.

One of the biggest differences working at The Open Championship, compared to the likes of The Wales Open or The English Open, was the fact that the top players in the world were there – a 'Who's Who' of the current golfing elite at the time. I'll never forget seeing Ernie Els close up and being taken by his size – a strapping individual with a languid swing that had earned him the nickname 'The Big Easy!' When he willingly agreed to let me take his photograph, at six foot four myself, I was eye-to-eye with a wonderful specimen of a sportsman and a previous winner of the Claret Jug. Many amateur golfers could learn a lot from his almost lazy swing, which still delivered long-distance drives. I later encountered Greg Norman – a past winner at Royal St George's – and was delighted when he agreed to let me take his photograph.

On Day 1 of the competition, I stood by the first tee as Tiger drove his ball into the rough on the right-hand side of the fairway. After the regulation five minutes allowed for looking for one's ball, Tiger's ball had not been located and he was buggied back to the tee to hit another ball. He holed out for a seven, not the start he had been looking for, I'm sure. The conditions were so terrible that the strong winds blew the roof off the television commentary box by the eighteenth green. Conditions had improved by the Saturday when sun cream was the order of the day.

Doug (arrowed)watches as Tiger Woods tees off at the 1st Hole

The search for Tiger's ball proves fruitless

Having got to know Mark McNulty quite well, and his wife Alison, who often walked the course while he was playing, I recall standing close to the 12th green and spotting Mark approaching. Having putted out, Mark and his playing partner headed off to the next tee. As he passed me, he said, "Hi, Doug. How are you?" He was off before I could reply. Like many Welsh people I have met in my business days, "How are you?" is a greeting, not a question! One of my nephews, Gary, was in the crowd at the time and made a comment about me knowing all the players.

Of course, I enjoyed that air of being known by professional golfers and relished the thought. The next player to walk off that same green was Nick Price – a previous Open Champion – and Gary whispered to me, "I guess you know Nick as well." It was said with a hint of sarcasm, but the truth was that I had never met Nick Price in the short time I had been a volunteer. However, Nick Price is an extremely friendly gentleman and, having putted out first, he came and stood by me. He turned to me and said, "Hi there. How are you today?" Again, he was another who walked off before I had an opportunity to reply, but he had given the impression that we were old buddies. Gary's face was a picture!

Later that day, I noticed a cameraman with a huge telephoto lens that looked about two feet long! Being interested in photography, I started chatting to him about his equipment and asked if I could have a look through his view finder. He willingly obliged and I saw Greg Norman walking towards the green in front of us. Although Greg was approximately one hundred metres away, his image filled the screen and the photographer let me press the shutter release. It was a great thrill for me to see one of the giants of game in such close up particularly as he was a previous winner of the Claret Jug on this very course.

The photographer then explained to me that the image would be transmitted straight from his camera to his office in London so that the image could be printed in that afternoon's sports report in the Evening Standard! How technological advances had eased the conveying of photographs from major sporting events was of great fascination to me. Long gone were the days of grubbing around in a dark room to find the best image to print!

One of the other scoring marshals had asked me if I had seen inside the Press Centre as it was quite easy to gain access, given that we were wearing Unisys outfits and they were the company handling all scoring information. My friend told me that the set-up was very impressive with many foreign golfing correspondents working on their reports for their journals or newspapers. It was an experience that I ought to try.

As I had Saturday afternoon off – my scoring duties were undertaken in the morning – I wandered over to the Press Centre, where a chunky security man stood guard at the entrance door. I simply smiled at him and walked straight into the building. Although this was within a cordoned off area – to which I had access with my marshal's pass – it was clearly necessary to stop any intruders making their way into this secure building. Once inside, I was fascinated to see about two hundred members of the press working away on their laptops while watching golf action on large TV screens in front of them. I heard an announcement saying that the tee times for the final day's play had been printed and were available at the central desk.

I wandered over to the desk and picked up a bundle of copies which I then distributed around the various reporters, who were hard at work with their heads down. They were all pleased to receive the information without having to leave their stations. Indeed, I blended in quite well and no one seemed to bother about this stranger in their midst. I then noticed there was an area in the corner that was curtained off by a lightweight material but a very bright light behind showed that something was going on behind that screen. No one seemed interested as I walked up to the curtains, successfully making my way through without doing an impression of Eric Morecambe on stage.

I found myself in a kind of studio where I had entered at the rear; at the front was a long desk behind which Thomas Bjorn was answering questions from approximately forty or fifty journalists about how he would handle the following day's play as he was the overnight leader at The Open Championship with one round to play. I took an available seat near the rear. There were two very attractive young girls hovering in the side aisles with microphones to pick up any questions from the floor. I smiled at the nearest girl, as you do, and to my surprise she approached me and stuck the microphone under my chin! "What is your question?" asked the interviewer sitting next to Thomas.

Imagine my surprise! I blurted out, "Doug Fowler – Henbury Telegraph" and Thomas looked at me while I asked a banal question about what his routines would be on the final day. Thomas explained that he would do nothing different as Royal St George's was a course that demanded respect and he had to be patient. Goodness knows how he kept his patience the following day when he bogeyed Par 3 on the 16th Hole and effectively handed the Claret Jug to newcomer Ben Curtis!

I thanked him for his answer and quickly left the way I had come in before I got into any trouble for faking it as a journalist! When I got back outside the Press Centre, I had to pinch myself that I had really done what I just did! I reported this incident in the Henbury Golf Club's monthly magazine when I returned home the following Monday.

This is the text of that report (which is basically a paraphrase of the above paragraphs):

"In July 2003 I was working as a volunteer marshal at The Open for the first time. The tournament was played at Royal St. George's, Sandwich in Kent.

My job was to work on a leader board by the 12th Green and it was great fun as we worked the four competition days on a rota basis, leaving me plenty of time to watch the golf. As I had the Saturday afternoon off – having worked in the morning – I ventured into the Press Centre late in the day. Interestingly enough, I was not challenged at the door by the security man as our uniform included a polo shirt with the 'Unysis" logo on the chest and he probably thought I was part of the media crew! (Unysis were responsible for the scoring system).

Once inside the centre, I was fascinated to see about two hundred correspondents from all over the world – working busily on their laptops to convey the latest news to their various headquarters. I heard an announcement reporting that the draw for the final round had been finalised and copies were available on the central desk. I went and picked up about fifty copies and busied myself distributing them to the grateful press journalists who were happy not to have to leave their workstations.

I then noticed that there was a section of the Press Centre that was curtained off with a translucent voile type material. Out of curiosity, I wandered over and had a peep inside. Imagine my surprise when I found myself in the middle of a press interview with the Danish golfer – Thomas Bjorn – who was leader in the clubhouse after three rounds. Addressing approximately forty journalists, he was taking questions from the floor. I sat down near the back of the room to listen and a gorgeous young woman with a 'roving microphone' came towards me. I smiled politely – as you do – and, to my utter amazement she handed me the microphone!

Somewhat taken aback, I blurted out – "Doug Fowler – Henbury Telegraph" the proceeded to ask Thomas – "What does it feel like to be on the eve of possible winning your first Major Championship?" To be fair, Thomas answered the question – and the journalists were all scribbling their shorthand notes – by saying that he was very excited but would do nothing differently because he had been advised to be patient when playing a challenging course like Royal St George's. I thanked him for his answer, wished him luck and made a speedy exit back out through the doorway through which I had entered a few minutes before!

Earlier in the week I met Ben Curtis and, although I had never seen or heard of him before, I took a photograph of him as he proudly told me he was from the US of A!

The rest is history!"

Following my hasty exit from the Press Centre, I found out about Mark Roe's unfortunate disqualification after he and Jesper Parnevik had failed to swap cards, thereby marking their own card which meant instant disqualification.

I'll never forget his philosophical response to an interviewer bluntly asking how he felt (why do they ask such dull questions?). He responded that disappointed though he was, golf was only a game and had nothing like the importance of his family and friends. They were such fine words given that he would have been in contention to win The Open Championship on the following day.

After leaving the Scorers' Headquarters one day, I noticed Gary Player walking by, accompanied by a giant security man. I politely asked Gary if I could take his photograph, but the security man raised his arm and said that Mr Player didn't stop for photographs. Gary Player said that, as I had asked in a courteous manner, he'd let me take his picture and I did. It is one of my prized possessions as Gary signed the photograph for me when I met him at St Andrews in 2005.

The long journey home from Sandwich was a surprisingly enjoyable experience as I was able to reflect on the past week and the excitement of having served at an event which had such wide appeal.

A few months after the event, I received letters from Steffi and Alice (my fellow scoreboard operators) asking for a reference from me as they had enjoyed the event so much that they were applying to do the same job at The Open next year at Troon. It was wonderful to hear from them and I duly obliged by writing a letter of commendation which was an easy task, as they had been first-class in carrying out their duties at Sandwich. I had sent them both a disk with all the photographs that I had taken when we were working together, and they appreciated my taking the trouble to do so. Happy memories.

CHAPTER 6 (2004)
THE WALES OPEN & THE BRITISH MASTERS

In 2004, The Wales Open was won by Simon Khan (Eng.), who beat Paul Casey in a play-off. As was his wont, Sir Terry Matthews very generously laid on a party for all marshals after the final day's play. The party was held in the hospitality structure by the 18th green, and it was fascinating to watch the catering staff clear the space in readiness for us. Some of us decided to have a bunker competition and see who could affect the most adventurous escape from one of the greenside bunkers. I think the competition was won by a lovely young girl, Lucy, who was a promising golfer and very handy with a sand wedge. Her dad – Nick – is in the photo below when I accompanied three other senior marshals on our complimentary round of golf at Celtic Manor, Westwood Hills Course.

When the room was cleared, we were faced with a mountain of food and drink, which we got stuck into with some relish. Sir Terry came into the building with the winner, and after a short speech of thanks, he went round table by table to thank us all personally for our hard work during the week. This was a gesture that was much appreciated by all the marshals, and it was a lovely touch to see Simon Khan also go table to table, with the trophy in his possession. He was happy to pose for photographs and let us have a brief hold of the Wales Open Trophy.

Doug with Wales Open Trophy

Doug with Simon Khan – winner of the 2004 Wales Open

When I was working at The British Masters at the Forest of Arden, I decided to stay locally overnight and booked into a B&B in Meriden; it wasn't cheap, but it was very convenient. It was just as well it was only one night because, as usual, golf tournaments usually result in all prices being hiked when golf is in town. After my duties ended at about 6:30pm, I made it back to the B&B where I changed quickly and headed over the road to the pub just opposite, where I had agreed to meet a couple of the other marshals for a meal. I think a hot meal after a hard day's work is one of life's real pleasures. If the food can be washed down with a few drinks in the convivial company of good friends, even better.

We had no sooner finished out meal than in breezed Ian Woosnam and Renton Laidlaw, the TV golf commentator, looking for somewhere to sit. Of course, we invited them to join us at our table and they immediately engaged us in conversation about the day's play. We drank and chatted until well past midnight as it seemed the landlord was infamous for his 'lock ins'. I eventually made it across the road to my B&B at about 1am, slightly worse for wear! I headed straight for the ensuite and sat on the toilet where I promptly fell sound asleep.

I woke at just after 4:30am, just in time to prepare for heading off to the golf course to start my early morning duties. I changed into my 'uniform' and crept quietly out of the B&B, spurning breakfast as it certainly wouldn't be available at that early hour. On my way to the golf course, I contemplated how I would tell my buddies in Aberdeen that I had paid £85.00 for a room and hadn't even slept in the bed!

I mentioned before the allocation of vouchers which were given to all marshals at the start of the day, for use in the tented village to buy lunch or whatever. At this venue, it was announced that the vouchers could not be exchanged for items in the pro shop, and we were to use them for food only. On the Saturday, a friend of mine said his wife had called him to return home because one of their children was poorly. He had collected about thirty vouchers and, on hearing that they could no longer be exchanged for golf equipment, he wasn't sure what he was going to do with such a number.

"Leave it to me," I said.

I wasn't intending to have a slap-up meal with all that money's worth. No, I decided that I would adopt the role of a philanthropist and distribute the excess vouchers among the paying public. On the Sunday morning, before going out with my match later, I wandered around the tented village looking for anyone that I thought would be deserving of these 'freebies'. It is, perhaps, a sad reflection on our modern society that most people stopped me the moment I said, "Excuse me, this is your lucky day as I have something to give you – for free!"

Comments such as "There's no such thing as a free lunch!" and "What are you selling?!" rained down and I found it extremely difficult to give these vouchers away even though I explained that they would have no value after that date. It took me quite a while to distribute all my excess vouchers and I ended up interrupting people in the food queues to hand them over. I would never have imagined that the job would be that difficult.

Ronnie O'Sullivan with Doug   **Angel Cabrera with Doug**

For the first time in my scoring career, I was given the last match to score and the pairing was the late Barry Lane (England) and Angel Cabrera (Argentina), one of the longest hitters on the circuit. Barry had represented Europe at the Ryder Cup Matches in 1993 but unfortunately lost all three of his matches. Nevertheless, he was playing really well in this final round.

It was a tight finish, but Barry produced the shot of the day on the 17th hole, which is a dogleg left to the right over water in front of the green. Barry's drive had failed to make the fairway when he tried to cut the corner and his ball ended up in some light rough around the inside corner of the fairway. A marshal was still looking for his ball when we arrived at the spot where his ball had landed. However, the bunker raker found it and, on close inspection, it was a horrible lie with the ball nestling down in the grass.

Somehow, Barry hit the most incredible recovery shot which flew across the water as we watched with our hearts in our mouths. His ball stopped about twenty feet from the pin, and he sank the putt, thus extinguishing any last hopes held by the gallant Argentinian. As we were leaving the 18th

green, with Barry confirmed as the winner and a three-shot margin of victory, he shook my hand in appreciation and signed his glove for me as a gift. What a gentleman and one of the humblest in the game of golf.

It was with real sadness that I read of his untimely death at the age of 62 in January 2023 and messages of sympathy around the world of golf demonstrated how well respected and loved he was. I for one feel blessed that I had the privilege of knowing him if even for only a brief period. He was one of golf's real gentlemen.

One of the worst overnight experiences I had was in a converted garage which had been recommended by one of the marshals. He told me it was a brilliant place to stay and remote from the house, so the owners wouldn't disturb me during the night – why should they? When I got to the accommodation, I found it was a concrete block garage – no insulation – and the 'building works' or conversion had been carried out by the owner who was a DIY enthusiast. The somewhat damp concrete floor was thinly disguised by a cheap, threadbare carpet. The 'ensuite' was a three-foot square erection in the corner of the garage where the door had to be left open if I wanted to sit on the throne. It was also classed as a 'wet room' which meant that operating the shower soaked everything in the space, including the towel and toilet paper! It was clear that the marshal who recommended this place had different values to mine. I stayed for one night only.

CHAPTER 7 (2005)
THE WALES OPEN & THE OPEN (ST ANDREWS)

At the Wales Open in 2005, a couple of scoring marshals – Peter Galliers and I – were asked if we minded trialling a new piece of kit which basically used GPS to accurately locate golf balls on the course. Of course, we readily agreed and did some field trials which were to be analysed and presented to the European Tour organisers as the way forward in scoring development. We were to use it on practice days and at the competition itself which, due to the Ryder Cup preparations for the Twenty Ten Course at Celtic Manor, was played on the Roman Road course.

We were briefed by the owners of the company 'Optimize Golf' and familiarised ourselves with the new kit – a handheld computer which could plot exactly where the ball was located at any point on the course. Initially, we stood at average driving distance on the first cut of rough and then walked out to where the ball landed on the fairway (or indeed the rough!) and pressed a button which accurately positioned the ball on the built-in GPS facility. We were given a free-ranging brief to try out the equipment on all parts of the course, particularly on the lower holes just to check that the signal was working OK in that more remote area of the golf course.

At one point, as Peter and I walked along, we caught up with Sir Nick Faldo, who was practising on his own with his caddie by his side. We asked if he minded us following him for a few holes and he was quite happy with that. When we explained what we were doing, Sir Nick took a keen interest in the equipment. Standing approximately 150 yards from a green, he asked me to tell him the exact distance to the pin. I read off that the distance and it was 148 yards.

Sir Nick turned to his caddie and said, "What do you make it?" His caddie said 145 yards – in other words, slightly shorter than what was showing on my screen. Sir Nick hit his ball, which landed three yards short of the pin! Realising that our equipment was giving more accurate information than his caddie, Sir Nick asked if the device could carry clubs?! His caddie wandered off ahead, shaking his head as he walked away from us.

My friend Peter had the pleasure of using the equipment 'in anger' on the final round when he walked with Miguel Angel Jiménez. It was a historic round as Miguel broke the course record with a fabulous 62!

Optimize Golf didn't succeed in persuading the European Tour officials that the system was robust enough to be adopted as their scoring system of choice. However, their Managing Director, Ian Ratcliffe, did send us both a beautiful print showing the record-breaking round of Miguel Angel Jimenez together with the scorecard as a 'thank you' for our services in testing their equipment.

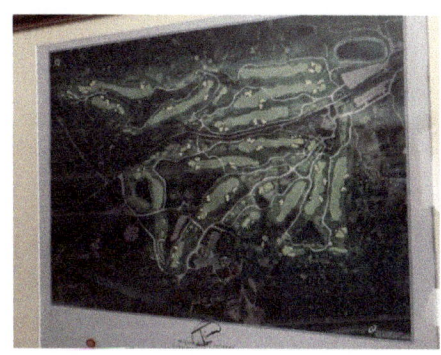

Miguel Angel Jimenez's record round at Celtic Manor   **Miguel Angel Jimenez**

There is a follow-up tale to receiving that fabulous gift as I wanted Miguel to autograph the print before I got it framed. Not an easy task with a print that is approximately three feet wide by two and a half feet high! I asked Peter if he would like me to obtain a signature on his print as well and he agreed.

I rolled both prints into a stout cardboard tube which I took with me to the next event to be held at The Belfry. I went into The Belfry Hotel just before breakfast, walked up to the reception desk and asked to see Miguel Angel Jiménez, who I knew was staying there for the duration of the event. The receptionist asked if I had an appointment and I replied that I had something that he really needed to see.

With that, the receptionist typed out a message that was relayed to Miguel's room, reading "Doug Fowler is in Reception and would like to meet you". As I have mentioned several times before, one must have a brass neck to get what you want in these situations.

Surprisingly, she said that he'd agreed to meet me in the foyer. Sure enough, after I had a nervous wait of about twenty minutes, Miguel appeared looking dapper as ever with highly polished brown leather shoes which really caught my attention. I was seated when he arrived. I jumped up to attention and said that I wanted to show him something. In that lovely voice of his he explained that he was about to have breakfast with his family, but he would come back and see me afterwards. As I was waiting, Peter Alliss appeared at the desk to check out, but I resisted interrupting him and asking for an autograph. He looked like he was busy with a call on his mobile phone at the time and wouldn't take to an interruption right at that moment.

Miguel duly reappeared about forty minutes later and asked what this was all about.

I opened the cardboard tube and unrolled the magnificent print onto the top of the grand piano in the reception area. Miguel was absolutely fascinated with the presentation map of the course, featuring all his shots – all 62 – recorded precisely in this format. He said, "Thank you. That is wonderful!" I panicked as I realised that he thought I was giving the print to him! I explained that I would like him to autograph the print for me as I was sure that he would be presented with a better-quality record of his achievement. He smiled that engaging smile, took my pen and signed right across his name in the middle of the print.

Wonderful, I thought as I rolled my print up to reveal Peter's copy below. Miguel laughed as he realised that I did indeed have a copy for him under my copy. I quickly explained that it was for a friend and reminded him of the scorer on the day of his record round. He willingly signed Peter's copy as well and congratulated me on my success in finding him and getting him to sign. That print is now framed and hangs proudly on my wall, right in front of me, as I write this.

At The Wales Open, when I was walking around the course on one of the practice days, I encountered a group of about twenty children who, it transpired, were over from Rednal Hill Junior School in Birmingham. They were refreshingly polite, because young children tended to be very pushy at golf events, asking players for autographs, balls, or any part of their equipment! These children were accompanied by an adult who turned out to be their headteacher and I could see that they weren't having much success in obtaining autographs from players. So, I offered to take one of their documents – a map of the course (see photograph below) – and use my influence to get some autographs for them which I duly did. I got signatures from Colin Montgomerie, Ian Woosnam, Sam Torrance, Lee Westwood, Paul Broadhurst, Sam Torrance and a few others.

I had to write the names of the golfers on a copy of the document so that the children could identify all the autographs.

When I returned the document to the headteacher, he was overjoyed and later wrote a lovely letter to me, thanking for taking the trouble to help. I was touched by their gratitude; it just goes to show the importance of communication with spectators. The headteacher's lovely letter included an invitation to visit their school and play their Par-3 course which had been constructed by the children with the proviso that I had to use the same clubs as those used by the children. I never did manage to take up the offer, but I mused at the prospect of such a tall man bending over to swing tiny golf clubs! Talking of tiny men, I'll never forget meeting the wonderful Ronnie Corbett CBE who played in the Pro-Am – he was a real delight and happy to pose with members of the public and volunteers alike. Whilst – at 6'-4" – I normally towered over most people that I meet, I have on occasions been overshadowed by tall security men.

Doug with the late Ronnie Corbett CBE

Tall security man with Doug   and another!

At The Open Championship later that year, it was my first experience of St Andrews. I had received my acceptance letter in January with confirmation that I was to attend the course on Wednesday 13th July when I would be allocated the location of the Scoreboard that I would be operating for the week. I had met a lovely man from St Andrews when I worked at Sandwich in 2003 and he had told me that he always worked the Scoreboard by the 1st Green at The Open. I gave him a call and he said that he would do what he could to get me a job alongside him, but it didn't work out that way as I was allocated a location by the 4th Hole. Nevertheless, I called by the Scoreboard where my friend was working, and we had a good chat about the excitement of seeing Jack Nicklaus playing there for the last time. I'm ashamed to say that I have forgotten his name and cannot find any reference to him or his lovely wife – such is the reality of the ageing process!

In the acceptance letter there was a note about our having to wear "normal golf clothing preferred" as tee shirts were no longer to be provided. The following paragraph read: "However, you will be provided with an Open Championship baseball cap at the briefing session." Obviously, costs were tight at this latest hosting of the great event.

Working at St Andrews wasn't a problem accommodation-wise as I could stay with my good friends Bob and Moira Cameron, who lived in Lundin Links which was only twelve miles west of St Andrews. Indeed, I recall my first trip to the course when I waited for a bus on the main road, and it duly arrived bang on time. When I showed my bus pass to the driver, he turned up his nose and said that it didn't work in Scotland! The fare was quite reasonable, and the bus depot was just off the City Road and only a few hundred yards from the Old Course. Using public transport, apart from the waiting around after the day's work, was a great advantage compared to the pain of parking at an allocated car park that was some distance from the course.

Doug and Bob Cameron (circa 1985)

Doug and Moira Cameron

Doug and Bob (recent)

I have to say here that my good friends, Bob and Moira, have been absolute bricks throughout my life, attending both my weddings and staying loyal throughout a fairly difficult couple of divorces! Bob and I went to school together and we have remained lifelong friends. They are both very keen golfers and Bob has worked at The Open Championship as a marshal where the individual holes are allocated to local golf club members. It is a system that works well.

The first photograph of Bob and me is there simply because of the amusing incident when his daughter, Fiona, asked – "Was that photograph taken when you were wee?!" Also, it is one of the rare photographs of me without a beard. In the more recent photograph of Bob and me, he seems to have grown – or I have shrunk a little! The photographs were taken at Lundin Golf Club which is in Lundin Links – I think that the names should be the other way round but there you go! I have also included a photograph of Bob with me, and Douglas Davidson taken on Lundin Golf Course at a hole called 'Perfection' – the fourteenth hole, a Par 3, which has the fairly unique distinction that all the other greens on the course are visible from that tee. I'm not sure that exists at any other golf course in the world.

Doug, Bob and Douglas Davidson on the tee at "Perfection" – the fourteenth hole at Lundin Golf Club

Douglas Davidson was introduced to me by Bob and Moira when I visited them in Lundin Links. We played golf together and, as we were chatting, I discovered that Douglas had been in charge of the distillery on the isle of Arran which I had visited on the New Year's Day of the Millennium. He, and his wife, Liz once prepared a barbecue in my honour when I travelled all the way north for my volunteering stint at The Open Championship. It was wonderful to receive such a warm welcome after a ten-hour drive.

Moira looked after me very well during The Open Championship, ensuring that I was well fed and that my clothes were all dried out in readiness for the following day. When my golf shoes had an absolute soaking one day, Moira cleverly packed the insides with newspaper to absorb the damp – it worked wonders.

Arriving for the first time in St Andrews, I was aware of a mounting air of anticipation and excitement about the place, in all its glory with the huge iconic yellow leader boards and grandstands surrounding the 18th green. The hairs on the back of my neck stirred when I walked down Golf Place and ventured along The Links where I first saw the majestic Headquarters of the R&A dominating a familiar scene that had witnessed so many dramas over its long history. It was hard to believe that the golf course was so much 'in the town' and turning a corner I was suddenly captured by its magnificence.

Doug standing by the 1st green at St Andrews – the Home of Golf

Doug with John Daly's golf bag

When I first visited the Scorers' Headquarters, I noticed quite a few familiar faces. Many of the volunteers worked at the event no matter where it was held, and it felt like a large family reunion. I felt really at home in this group. I stood proudly by the first green to have my photograph taken before catching up with John Daly during one of his practice rounds. I had my photograph taken standing by Big John's golf bag and it amused me to see that there was a special compartment for his beer glass!

I was to be working in a greenside scoreboard by the 4th hole, so I strolled out there straight away to assess my home for the next few days. I've never quite understood why but we were paid the princely sum of £150.00 for volunteering at that event, whereas it was normally unpaid at lesser

European Tour events. Indeed, I would have willingly paid that amount for the privilege of viewing golf from 'inside the ropes'. Payment involved standing in a long queue at the Royal Bank of Scotland's kiosk in the Tented Village.

I have previously described the internal layout of the hut where the players' names and scores numbers were located for efficient loading of the display boards on the front of the hut. When the board was lowered, to allow us to change the names, etc., it revealed a long slot which was a bit like a low window opening, approximately five feet wide.

Paul Casey played an approach shot on the second day, he pulled it left and it came into our hut through one of these narrow slot windows! After bouncing around inside, his ball eventually came to rest on top of our 'red numbers' (which indicate under par scores) next to No.8. It was frightening to be inside the hut with a golf ball bouncing around at speed – like being inside a pinball machine! Thankfully, the girls were outside on the viewing platform at that moment, and I managed to 'dodge the bullet'. When Paul came into the hut with the walking referee, I quipped that he had just gone to eight under par! He wasn't amused. Of course, he got a free drop nearby and successfully hit his shot stone dead.

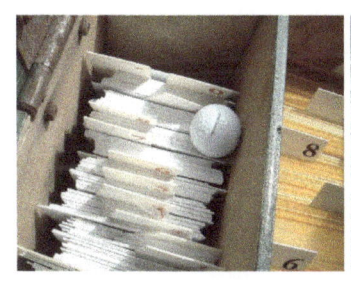

Paul Casey's ball landed in storage box

Doug preparing to load names on to leader board display

I recall watching several top golfers hitting their balls into the greenside bunker at the front left-hand side of the green near where our hut was situated, so we had a first-class view of the various methods of getting out of the sand. Most players avoided the threat posed by the steep face of the bunker and they would bale out left where their balls often ran on to the 14th green (St Andrews is renowned for its shared greens). However, I saw Sergio Garcia take his stance in the sand and open his club before hitting a sublime flop shot which rolled on to the green and finished about ten inches from the hole.

My experience in that leader board hut was not the best as the performance of some of the other volunteers was well below the standard that I had experienced at Sandwich in 2003. Unfortunately, some volunteers saw their jobs as a free ticket to watch golf and I fell victim to this attitude when I went off for my lunch break and returned to find all the players' names – on the long plastic strips that were threaded into slots on the leader board – scattered all around the floor of the hut! The normal procedure, after each group had passed that point, was to put all the names in alphabetical order back in the large storage box at the back of the hut. In addition, two of the volunteers spent most of their time as spectators, watching the golf.

I was so annoyed that I wrote to the Chief Scorer and said that I wouldn't work with such idiots again in the future. They were sacked as a result, but they deserved what they got. It is a great privilege to work 'inside the ropes' and The Open Championship is the most professionally run tournament of all. Our scoring duties meant that we all had to be on the ball, as it were.

To commemorate Jack Nicklaus's illustrious career, the Royal Bank of Scotland issued a special five-pound note that year and these were available in the bank's pavilion in the Tented Village. I waited until the queue was quite short and made my way to the counter where I enquired how many I could purchase. I was told that the maximum was ten and I'll never forget the teller's expression when I asked how much that would cost.

"Well, fifty pounds. What did you expect?!"

I had been convinced that there would be a premium on these items which would inevitably make their way on to eBay.

The front of the £5 note was largely the same as the existing Royal Bank of Scotland £5 notes, apart from the fact the Golden Bear logo is shown and that the serial number only appears once. In addition, all the serial numbers for this commemorative banknote commence with 'JWN', short for Jack William Nicklaus. The reverse of the banknote was completely redesigned and showed images of Jack holding the Claret Jug and playing a shot during his way to victory at St Andrews in 1978. The R&A clubhouse is depicted on the top left-hand portion of the note and in the bottom left, Jack's winning scores at St. Andrews in 1970 (when he won an 18-hole play-off with Doug Sanders) and in 1978 are depicted. On the bottom right-hand side of the note, the tee at the 18th hole can be seen along with the Swilken Bridge.

Jack was interviewed by the BBC, and he said that it was such an honour, and he couldn't believe that the bank would place a 'foreigner' on their bank notes. Such was the humility of the man. He was quoted as saying, "A career in golf would be incomplete if it didn't include a win at The Open Championship at St Andrews, the Home of Golf!"

My collection of RBS commemorative five-pound notes

Indeed, I gather that a spectator asked Jack to autograph one of the newly printed notes, assuring him that it was for his personal collection. It appeared on eBay the very next day for a vastly inflated price and Jack, quite rightly, refused to sign any more once he realised that he had been duped. Of the ten that I purchased, I gave away several to my golf-playing brothers and close golfing friends while I retained the others in my collection of golfing memorabilia. I believe their value is considerably more than £5.00 each now!

It was always my ambition to obtain an autograph from Jack Nicklaus as he had been another golfing hero of mine. I had a great opportunity while waiting outside the R&A Headquarters one afternoon. I saw Jack walking towards the collection point where players were taken by limousine to their hotel, and he was talking to Tom Watson. However, I had prepared a special document for Tom to sign (which was to be a gift, commemorating his victory in The Open at Troon in 1982, for an old friend of mine at Henbury Golf Club in Bristol) and this was a golden opportunity for me to obtain both autographs as there was no one else around to crowd me out. Unfortunately, when Tom stopped to tell me that he wasn't signing autographs, Jack decided to turn round and head back into the building.

Realising that I had lost my chance, I walked alongside Tom and explained that I wanted him to sign something special. To be fair to the great man, he stopped and looked at the document I held out to him. Having read it, he said, "It will be my pleasure to sign." I was so thrilled, and I knew how much it would mean to my friend, John Brewer, when he learned that I'd manage do speak to his hero. The background to this little story is that John was Captain of Henbury Golf Club in 1982 – the year that Tom won The Open at Troon – and he had introduced a new trophy competition to the club. I believe that the Troon Trophy is still played for at Henbury Golf Club to this day.

When I returned to Henbury Golf Club the following week, the current captain had the document framed and presented it to John in the clubhouse. When he looked at Tom Watson's signature – and best wishes – he broke down in tears of joy. I realised at that moment that I had made the right decision, albeit I didn't get an autograph from Jack Nicklaus.

John Brewer
Henbury Golf Club – Captain 1982

Tom Watson
Open Championship Winner 1982
Royal Troon

*To John
Best wishes
Tom Watson*

Tribute signed by Tom Watson

Jack Nicklaus posing on his final visit to St Andrews

As it was to be Jack's last appearance at The Open, he decided that it had to be at the Home of Golf and people turned out in their thousands to show their appreciation of the great man. It was an emotional final day for Jack when he played on the Friday with Tom Watson, and I'll never forget seeing them hug by the 18th green. Saying goodbye to their old adversary was still a moment to savour for the pair of them.

I sent a letter to Jack Nicklaus some years later at his home in Florida, asking if he would sign my £5.00 note on the basis that the clamour to sell these had probably died down. He politely declined but did me the honour of signing a photograph of himself on his final crossing of the Swilken Bridge, so I was satisfied. That photograph hangs on the wall in front of me right now, inscribed "To Doug, With Best Wishes, Jack Nicklaus" – a wonderful memento. He did return my £5.00 note as well.

The Open Championship was won that year by Tiger Woods, who led from Day 1 and held off the challenges of both José Maria Olazábal and Colin Montgomerie, who had given all Scots the hope of a possible local winner. It wasn't to be for Colin but the support for him was immense, eclipsed only by the public's admiration of Tiger's tenacity and determination. He won by the widest margin since his previous win in 2000 with a score of sixteen under par.

It was another memorable week and, not only did I see many top golfers, but I had also met a couple from Bristol with whom I had played golf many times; they were fans of The Open Championship and said how lucky I was to be involved in such a fabulous event. So true.

CHAPTER 8 (2006)
THE WALES OPEN, THE OPEN (HOYLAKE) & THE RYDER CUP (K CLUB)

This chapter could be called – 'That was the year that was!'

It was the most packed commitment that I had during my scoring career. Three tournaments in the space of six months – quite a challenging schedule but one that I was to happily undertake with pleasure.

I recall the Pro-Am day at Celtic Manor in 2006 when Barry Drew asked me to be a Walking Marshal with Michael Campbell (NZ) as his celebrity was going to be Ronan Keating, the former Boyzone singer. Perhaps because of my size and bulk, Barry saw me as being a suitable minder for Ronan around the course.

I was looking forward to meeting him as I was a fan and had seen him perform in Cardiff a couple of years beforehand. When I headed down to the first tee – they were playing the Roman Road course – I was surprised to see that there wasn't a throng around the place in anticipation of Ronan's arrival. Just as I got 'inside the ropes', Barry came over and told me that Ronan Keating was a 'no show' as he had pulled out of the event. However, in his place was the Welsh Rugby star, Ieuan Evans, a player that I had admired during the then Five Nations Rugby Championship.

I was introduced to Ieuan and Michael Campbell on the first tee along with a couple of amateur golfers, one of whom was part of the management team at Celtic Manor, who had paid a fee to play with this group. It was a very relaxed group, and I enjoyed the chat around the course. I took the opportunity to tell Ieuan how I secretly admired his marvellous try against my beloved Scotland Team in Cardiff in 1988, albeit I was gutted at the time. "One of my finest tries", he said as he described how he'd swerved past several Scottish defenders on his way to the try line! I knew, I had watched that try repeatedly.

One rather lovely incident was on the back nine when our group was playing the 17th Hole and Gareth Edwards was playing in a group on the adjacent fairway. Spotting Gareth, Ieuan shouted something (not very complimentary I'm sure) to him, and it was wonderful to experience that close bond that exists between sportsmen as they exchanged friendly banter. It also gave me the opportunity to get a photograph of Gareth Edwards, a true legend of the game of rugby and a lovely man besides.

In a quiet moment earlier on the tee to a Par-3 Hole, I overheard Michael Campbell asking Ieuan about rugby in the modern era and Ieuan pointed out that fitness was an important element now that stoppages had been reduced significantly. In Ieuan's time, he reckoned that they played about fifteen minutes of actual rugby whereas modern players had to play for at least twice that long. To be honest, I had noticed that while watching rugby on TV. It was also marvellous listening to top sportsmen discussing their individual sports and reflecting on the difference between rugby – a team game – and golf, which was very much an individual sport (except for the Ryder Cup Matches and the like).

At the end of the round, Ieuan thanked me for looking after him and I asked him if he would kindly say something into my camera (set to video) for my grandson, Ben, who was ten years old and had just taken up rugby. He was very generous and recorded a message wishing Ben good luck in his playing years ahead. A lovely touch and such a gentleman. I was thrilled at the prospect of passing his good wishes on to Ben.

My acceptance letter for The Open Championship that year was dated 3rd April, a good two months later in the year than previous championships, so there was less time to find suitable accommodation. A paragraph in the letter caught my attention immediately: "With the increased sophistication of the scoring system, it is essential that you attend one of the 'Teach-Ins' on the Sunday or the Monday." I was intrigued to find out how much more information the scoring system could handle, and I wasn't too surprised to find out that the golfing world required more 'stats' as the competition unfolded.

For the first time in my experience of the R&A, a little confusion had set in because I also received another letter advising me that I was successful in my application to work on a Scoreboard! I got on the phone immediately and said that I had already been selected as a Walking Scorer, albeit this was to be my first experience of the role that I had wanted to perform ever since my stint at Sandwich in 2003 (although I didn't say that during my telephone conversation!).

It seemed no time at all before I was heading up the M5/M6 to the Wirral and Hoylake.

My accommodation at Hoylake was an absolute delight. One of my friends, Moira Cameron, on hearing that I was struggling to find somewhere suitable, pointed out that local churches had come up with a scheme whereby congregation members would let out rooms in their houses. The initiative was called 'Wirral Churches Hospitality Scheme for The Open Championship' – the brainchild of one Reverend David Muir. The basis of the scheme was that congregation members would offer free accommodation in exchange for a £25.00 per night donation to their selected charities. With fifty thousand golf fans expected to turn up each day, this scheme proved extremely successful for volunteers, who had to pay for their own accommodation. It really was a win-win situation.

I got in touch with one of the local ministers and found a family willing to put me up for ten days. I'll never forget the family; the woman was called Priscilla Bench-Capon and she was extremely helpful, sending me a map of the town marked up with all the local hostelries, chemists, doctors' surgeries, etc. She really did go all out to make my visit as enjoyable as possible.

When I arrived, Priscilla showed me to my room, which was beautifully set out with a shared bathroom across the hall. Having previously advised her that I would be leaving early in the mornings so breakfast would not be required, she showed me into the kitchen where I would be welcome to make up sandwiches and the like.

When she opened the fridge door, I noticed there were several cans of beer which I thought was quite unusual for the people living in that house, being devout Christians and unlikely to indulge in alcoholic excesses, although I don't know what I based that assumption on. Priscilla pointed to the beers and said, "Those are for you. We understand that you golfers like a drink or two!"

Hallelujah! I had really landed on my feet!

There was huge media interest in this championship as The Open Championship hadn't been held at Hoylake since 1967 when Roberto De Vicenzo won and that was thirty-nine years before. I read a report that mentioned the total number of spectators in 1967 was thirty thousand whereas the R&A predicted thirty-five thousand spectators a day at Hoylake for this championship, such was the appeal of the event. Records show that over two hundred and thirty thousand spectators attended the event over the course of the four championship days. Also, Tiger Woods had lost his father only three months beforehand and the golfing world was intrigued to see how he would cope. Indeed, it was to be a very emotional week for Tiger.

This was my first experience as a Walking Scorer and, at the briefing session, I realised that the whole scoring process had stepped up a gear since my experiences running a Scoreboard in 2003. The company responsible for the scoring kit was an American company which also did the scoring at The Masters. We were briefed by a lovely Australian man, by the name of Ralus, and it was quite clear that scoring was going to be a whole lot more complicated than what I had experienced on the European Tour up to that point.

We were each handed a handheld scoring device (a minicomputer), which was explained to us in graphic detail. It was the first time that 'In the Hole' was appropriate in my view – I always hated hearing that phrase which idiots shouted from the crowd even on the first tee at a Par 5 hole! The training session took us through a few scenarios that were likely to happen on the course, such as the situation where a player had to play a provisional ball (one of the more complicated situations – that and a foul shot!). After the intensive training session, we were to go out on the course the following day and use the equipment while following players who were practising.

We had to be up to speed with our operation of the equipment, and a recording sheet of paper on a clipboard and a radio. I started to feel quite nervous at the prospect of conveying scoring information which was going to be relayed to millions of golf fans around the world in real time. Laxatives not required at this stage! However, 'every cloud has a silver lining' sprang to mind as I planned my 'on course' training the following day when I would choose a player that I liked to follow. Of course, nothing was left to chance and the on-course training was allocated to small groups of Walking Scorers who would accompany groups of players around the course. I often ignored this arrangement and walked out to where there was a player I wanted to see; not strictly the 'done thing' but I had some fabulous experiences when doing so.

During the round of golf, Walking Scorers were allowed to walk on the first cut of grass along fairways but not on the fairway itself, the point being that television cameras wanted to see as few people as possible around the golfers being filmed. Sometimes it was inevitable that we had to walk on the fairway to follow a player who maybe had strayed into the rough on the other side. On these occasions, I would advise the scoreboard carrier and the bunker raker to wait together to avoid our small group wandering all over the place.

The routine I adopted, which always proved to be effective, was to walk close to the Match Referee because he or she had to witness every shot being hit, as did the Walking Scorer. (The R&A had introduced the practice of putting a referee out with every game back in 1990.) This also helped when checking scores after the hole had been completed. For example, if a player's ball went into a deep greenside bunker, I had to position myself in a place where I could always see the ball. This sometimes led to a bit of dash to get to the exit point from the green before the on-course marshals closed off the ropes. I had narrowly avoided being garrotted on several occasions. I can remember times when the marshals were keen to open fairway crossings and they looked rather glum as our little group trailed at a discreet distance behind the players and their caddies.

After each round of golf, the players head straight for the R&A Recorder's Office, near the 18th Green, to scrutinise their cards before signing them and handing them in. Any errors at that stage can lead to disqualification – reference Mark Roe at the 2003 Open when he made an error on his scorecard by forgetting to swap with his playing partner, Jesper Parnevik! Mark would had been able to challenge for the trophy on the final day. Following that unfortunate incident, I know that Ivor Robson always made it clear that he was handing the other player's card to the golfer on the first tee.

Following completion of the round, as Walking Scorers we were shown to a seat in the corner of the Recorder's Office – known to scorers as 'the naughty chair' simply because one sits there in trepidation of being asked to clarify a situation if a player has a query! The scores that we had entered on our hand-held computers were shown on a screen above the heads of the R&A officials, so the players can refer to them if necessary. Quite intimidating when one considers the importance of our role in respect of these top players and their need to be certain that their scorecards were in good order.

Inside the Recorder's Office

On my first visit to the course, on Tuesday morning, I was around at about 6am when the BBC turned up in force to broadcast as part of their BBC Breakfast programme with Chris Hollins and Carol Kirkwood, the weather presenter. With no public around at that early hour, I was able to approach the two presenters and ask for photographs. They were so obliging, and we had fun as I was photographed alongside both and also individually. I explained to Carol that I would be the envy of my friend back in the gym at Bristol because we always watched her weather forecast during our gym routines.

Andy would shout, "Turn to BBC, Carol's presenting the weather!" We were both great fans. I told her that I would call Andy on my mobile phone there and then to tell him about meeting Carol. Indeed, I asked Carol if she would chat to my friend on my mobile. She was such a good sport, took my phone and, when Andy answered the call, she said, "Hello, Andy. How are you?"

I could hear his response as he struggled to work out who was on the phone at this early hour.

"Who's that?" he asked.

Carol went straight for the jugular and said, "Well, if you're going to play hard to get, I'm not going to join you with a bottle of Champagne when I visit Bristol."

Andy was dumbfounded and remarked that it couldn't really be THE Carol Kirkwood on my phone. He asked her to describe what she was wearing, which she did, and he, by that time, realised this was really happening and not part of some fantasy dream.

**Doug with Carol Kirkwood   Chris Hollins and Carol
– both with the BBC**

Carol on the phone to my friend

I thought that Carol was such a sport and I noticed that when the spectators started to arrive later, she was equally at ease, offering selfies and signing autographs. Andy dined out on that story for some time afterwards. I sent my photographs to the BBC and asked if Carol and Chris would sign them for me which they did soon afterwards.

Shortly after my encounter with Carol and Chris, I noticed Peter Dawson carrying a black plastic bin liner. I joked that he was probably carrying the Claret Jug in there and he replied that he was, saying that it was the best form of security. Peter was Chief Executive of the R&A at the time. He had walked out to be interviewed by the BBC and I was standing near a small group of BBC cameramen when he arrived.

On the basis that if you don't ask, you don't get, I asked him if I could be so bold as to be allowed to hold that magnificent trophy. He readily agreed and when I cheekily asked if he would take a photograph with my camera, he agreed saying that I was pushing my luck! I was really privileged to hold that famous trophy and I could see so many great names etched on the base – what a scoop! I have treasured that image ever since and baffled my friends by showing them the picture of me proudly holding the great trophy which is a privilege not normally accorded to members of the public let alone a high handicap golfer like me.

Peter Dawson with the Claret Jug   **Doug with the Claret Jug**

The weather conditions were variable that week with play being delayed by two hours on Day 1 because a predicted electrical storm was about to hit the Wirral. Then, on Day 2, it was so hot that emergency fire engines were brought to the course in case of fire.

I walked with Game No.26 on the Friday, my very first experience of being a Walking Scorer at The Open Championship. Unlike the Ryder Cup Matches, the whole atmosphere was less boisterous, and scoring was quite straightforward with the additional features simply requiring that we pinpoint where the ball lay before each stroke was made. When I returned to Scorers' HQ after my round, I was delighted to have successfully completed an incident-free round and Ralus was there to congratulate me as I handed in my handheld device and radio. I felt elated that I had contributed effectively to such an immense event in my own small way.

One of my golfing friends, Andy Besant – Captain of Henbury Golf Club at the time – gave me a drawing of Tiger Woods and asked me to get it signed by Tiger so that it could be auctioned off for charity. I made no promises as it is extremely difficult to get close to Tiger when he is around the golf course these days. I had the great idea of giving the drawing – in a presentation cardboard tube – to Steve Williams, Tiger's caddie, so that he would be more likely to get Tiger to do the deed. I saw Steve at the putting green and explained the situation to him. He said that the best thing for me to do was to give it to him and he'd get Tiger to sign it, after which he would leave it in the locker room.

Later in the day, I saw the Locker Marshal, who was a friend of mine, and asked him if the drawing had been signed by Tiger, but he said that was unlikely as Tiger didn't use the locker room. I never saw the drawing again despite requesting a search of the locker room. After my experience with Tiger at The Belfry in 2002, I was hoping to get his signature and make amends for our previous unfortunate encounter but that wasn't to be!

On Day 3, I walked with Robert Karlsson and Mark O'Meara (a past Open Champion). I had previously walked with Robert at The Wales Open but Mark O'Meara, being a previous champion, had an aura about him that seemed to elevate him above the others that I had accompanied. After the round, the players were checking their cards, when Mark got up and walked straight over to where I was sitting. I thought, *Damn! What have I done wrong?*

I immediately stood up and he reached out to shake my hand, saying, "Thank you for spending the past few hours with us; your help is greatly appreciated."

I think I visibly relaxed as he got out a brand-new golf ball and signed it before handing it to me and shaking my hand again.

I had always admired Mark, but this action was the sign of a class act. When I left the scorers' enclosure, I met Gareth Lord (Lordy), Robert Karlsson's caddy – with whom I have had a friendly relationship spanning several years – and I showed him the signed golf ball that Mark O'Meara had just given to me. It was the strongest hint I could give him that I would have liked Robert to do the same.

Gareth immediately realised that it would be better if I also had a signed ball from Robert. So, I hung around chatting to 'Lordy' (as he is affectionately known in golfing circles) for a few minutes while Robert spoke to his psychologist on his mobile telephone. Apparently, after a round, Robert would always call his psychologist to give him a 'de-brief' immediately. After finishing his telephone call, Robert came over and said hello. Gareth handed him a shiny new golf ball and asked him to sign it for me, which Robert did with pleasure. It's not what you know, it's who you know!

Golf Balls

signed by

Mark O'Meara (USA)

&

Robert Karlsson (Sweden)

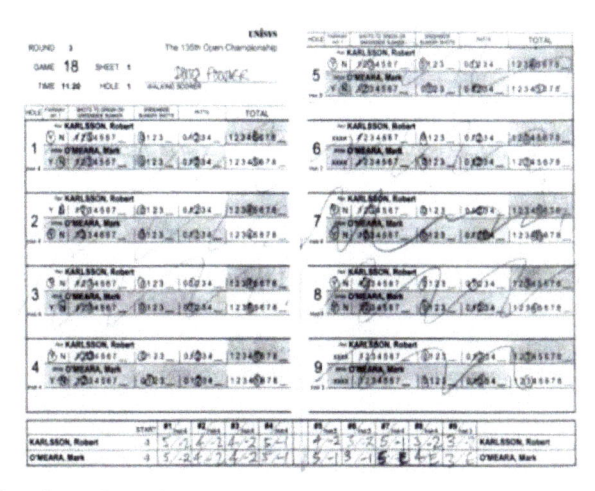

The signed golf balls and part of the scoresheets from that round

It was one of my most enjoyable days on the golf course, heightened by the sheer professionalism and courtesy shown by both Mark and Robert, and I had two signed golf balls to commemorate the experience. I kept my paper copies of the score sheets as a memento of a truly wonderful experience.

I was delighted to note that Gareth Lord was voted 'Caddie of the Year' in 2008 – a well-deserved accolade. Gareth would always say hello no matter where I bumped into him, even in the supermarket in Portrush where I saw him early one morning in 2019.

Tiger won The Open Championship that year and never once used woods; he played irons and picked his way around the course meticulously. His emotions burst to the surface after he was presented with the trophy as this was his first win since losing his father on whom he had come to rely so heavily in his earlier career.

I mentioned before about world-famous golfers being more approachable than footballers and this was highlighted when I came across Gary Lineker at The Open at Hoylake. He had taken on golf presenting for the BBC for some reason and could often be seen around the press area of the tented village. I was standing within the roped area, chatting to a couple of schoolboys who were clutching their autograph books, when he walked towards us with his head down reading some documents in his hand.

The boys were super-excited at the prospect of getting his autograph, but when he looked up from his papers and saw them, he turned on his heels and headed off in the opposite direction! He only had to walk a few more paces and make their day; there were no other autograph hunters around, so it wasn't as if he was going to be mobbed. The boys were deeply disappointed, and I doubt that Gary Lineker was held in such esteem by them thereafter!

One of the funniest things that I have ever experienced on a golf course was at Hoylake one afternoon when I was enjoying watching the golf during an afternoon off after my duties had been completed in the morning. Standing outside the ropes down the left-hand side of the first hole – we were encouraged not to abuse our passes by going inside the ropes when not on duty – I was suddenly aware of a conversation going on between two locals (Scousers) standing close to me. It was quite clear that they didn't really understand the game, so I couldn't resist asking them what had brought them to the course. One of them proudly said that his boss had given him two tickets as a gesture of goodwill, so here they were although they had never been to a golf tournament before. Indeed, one of them said that he had no idea what the game was all about because he had never seen it on TV or taken any interest in newspaper reports as he was a soccer fan himself.

I agreed to explain the basics of the game, which were that the objective was to hit the golf ball from the tee on our right all the way to the hole on the green way off to our left in as few shots as possible. I know that is a massive oversimplification of our beloved sport, but these guys took it in great spirit. Indeed, at that very point Miguel Angel Jiménez walked casually by, as he always does, down the middle of the fairway, puffing on a huge cigar. Miguel always walked in a very striking manner with his chest proudly stuck out in front of him and his ponytail threaded through the rear of his cap. On observing this casual vision of a middle-aged gentleman strolling past us, one of the Scousers said, "Now that's the kind of sport I'd like to play!"

In terms of humorous occurrences, I bumped into Ken Brown – famed for his 'On the Course' clips during the transmission of The Open Championship both when at The BBC and when working for Sky – when he was chatting to someone next to a green on one of the practice days. When there was a break in their conversation, I politely asked Ken if he would sign a photograph for me and he readily agreed. From somewhere in the deep reaches of my brain, out came the words, "I love your commentary, Ken – so much better than that bloke on Sky!"

As he handed me back my photograph, he gestured to the gentleman standing next to him and said, "This is that bloke from Sky!"

I was mortified as I just hadn't recognised him in the flesh.

Ken Brown MBE   **Chris Hollins's message**

Carol Kirkwood's message

Within a few weeks of The Open at Hoylake, I received a note from Carol Kirkwood in which she had signed the photographs of us together and that was shortly followed by a note from Chris Hollins with his autograph as well.

When it came to heading for home, I had had such a good time staying with that lovely family that I was happy to pay a substantial donation to the church funds. I left early on the last day and found a small square note had been pushed under my room door – it read:

"Goodbye, Doug. Have a good day and a safe journey home. God bless you. We liked having you to stay. Thank you for the donation. Priscilla and Trevor."

Such wonderful people.

However, my journey home turned out to be a nightmare of epic proportions! As I was driving out of the car parking field, across some corrugated aluminium sheeting that had been laid out to protect the ground and provide a stable foundation for traffic, a security person waved me to pull off to one side and allow a truck through. There was a terrific bang, and I stopped my car to check that all was OK. Luckily, or so I thought, all appeared to be OK, so I drove off to fill up with petrol for the return journey down the M6/M5 back to Bristol.

When I pulled into the filling station, I noticed that oil was dripping quite profusely from under the engine! It wasn't a garage, as I had hoped, and a Sunday wasn't a good day for sorting mechanical problems. To cut a long story short, I had to call the AA and they arrived some three hours later, hoisted my car onto their breakdown truck and ferried me back home. It wasn't the most comfortable ride home and, to make matters worse, the driver was coming to the end of his shift and needed to swap with another driver just outside Birmingham. I eventually made it home at 2am the following morning and my car faced a major repair.

Although I wrote to the car park people, they denied responsibility, saying there were warning signs around (although none stated, "Beware of Stupid Security Staff!") and I had to stump up – a sad end to a magnificent week.

The highlight of 2006, for me, was undoubtedly the Ryder Cup Matches played at The K Club in Straffan, County Kildare, near Dublin in Ireland. Indeed, the excitement had started way back in 2002 when I started looking for accommodation. This was always going to be difficult given that the Ryder Cup had never been played in Ireland before and the Americans would be over in their thousands, snapping up whatever accommodation was available at whatever cost.

I teamed up with Peter Galliers, a friend at Henbury Golf Club (Bristol), and we booked up a shared room at the Tulfharris Hotel & Golf Resort, near where the event was going to be held. We would be crossing by ferry from Fishguard to Rosslare and that was also booked up early on.

Travel arrangements:

Outward ferry – Fishguard to Rosslare departing Friday 15th September 2006 at 11:30, arriving at 13:30.

Passengers: 1 Adult and 1 Senior Citizen (I don't think Peter ever forgave me for pointing out that he was a little older than me!).

Return ferry – Rosslare to Fishguard departing Monday 25th September 2006 at 15:00, arriving at 17:00.

On reading that confirmation, I wondered what confusion would be caused if bad weather caused a delay in the event as had happened at The Open in 1988 when Seve Ballesteros won at Royal Lytham St Annes on Monday – the first time that happened in the championship's long history! Be careful what you wish for.

However, although I didn't work at the 2010 Ryder Cup at Celtic Manor, that event was delayed until the Monday due to heavy rain.

Either way, it was going to be a long journey back to Bristol late in the afternoon after a tiring few days of walking and scoring.

Our booking was confirmed on 4th January 2005, and it was good to know that our accommodation was all sorted – always a relief around such popular events. In fact, I recall the reservation in detail because, unusually, the reservation dates were from 2006–09–18 to 2006–09–25, which effectively meant 18th September to the 25th of September 2006. As usual, I was very careful with my administration as these things can't be left to chance.

I recall a conversation with my wife sometime after the event when her cousin, an avid golfer, was talking about the Ryder Cup being a three-day event and my wife asked me why I had to be there for ten days! Due time was required to soak up the atmosphere, play a few rounds of golf, attend training sessions, and accompany players while out on the course practising. All these activities had to be given a high level of attention as this was a global event and we would be working in front of the television cameras which would be transmitting the action to a massive audience.

Much to my surprise, however, I took a call from an Irish woman in August 2005 saying that she was just confirming our hotel room booking for the following month and how she was looking forward to seeing us soon. I had to double-check the year when I looked in my diary. In a sense of panic, I reached for my file and, sure enough, our bookings were for September 2006! In a very strong Irish brogue, the woman explained that we surely wouldn't be coming to their hotel in 2006 as that was when they were planning a complete refurbishment.

I pointed out that she must have gotten it completely wrong as no hotel in Ireland would close while the Ryder Cup was in town! This was a hospitality opportunity not to be missed by any organisation within striking distance of The K Club.

However, despite written confirmation that our booking was for a year later, she said that we had better make alternative arrangements. We scrambled to find somewhere suitable, and the Irish Chief Marshal put us in touch with a local B&B in nearby Hollywood where we did manage to find a room to share for the duration of our stay. Our complete bewilderment at the attitude of the hotel management was founded on the fact that they had probably bumped us off their list so that they could command more lucrative rates from the wealthy American visitors who would be coming over in their droves. To our utter amazement, when we visited the hotel in 2006 to check it out, it was indeed closed for refurbishment. Unbelievable!

After a calm ferry crossing, Peter and I arrived in Ireland on the Thursday before the Ryder Cup Matches were to be played, so that we could get a few games of golf in during our familiarisation period. Our B&B turned out to be a lovely Georgian house – called Knockrue House - on a working farm with a fantastic landlady called Eileen who insisted on getting up and serving us breakfast, albeit we would be leaving before 6 o'clock each morning. We shared a large room with an ensuite bathroom on the first floor where I think there were at least four other bedrooms with guests who had more 'normal' hours of occupation. We never saw them but heard movements during the night.

Our first trip to The K Club involved parking in a huge field nearby but several days of heavy rain had rendered it an absolute quagmire and we all got in a right mess. On top of that, there was a storm in the night resulting in trees falling all over the place and blocking our route to the course. This was not quite the experience that we had expected when we signed up for this event. Emergency arrangements were put in place to divert cars to Punchestown Racecourse from which we were taken by bus to the golf course. It was a remarkable feat of logistics and evidence that the tournament planners had done their preparatory work well. Thankfully, we had to report to the course early in the morning, so the place wasn't too busy when we made our way through the storm-damaged countryside.

Doug proudly standing on 1st tee at The K Club

As a result of the storm, there was an electrical blackout at the B&B, but it only lasted a few hours and power was restored quite quickly. One small fact that my roommate, Peter, failed to pass on to me was the fact that the power cut had resulted in the failure of the small pump which filled the water cistern in the roof – he was advised to be sparing with the use of showering water to conserve what little there was. I was in the shower, having lathered shampoo all over my head, when the water supply slowed to a trickle. I called out to Peter that I was in a mess, and he simply replied. "Oh yes, we need to be sparing with the water – didn't I tell you?!"

Of course, he hadn't. Getting shampoo out of one's hair without an ample supply of water is an activity I wouldn't want to repeat as I had 'stiff hair' for the rest of that day! Peter simply chuckled with that little laugh of his; he was like that, often winding me up with his little pranks.

Doug and Peter relaxing after a hard day's work

Knockrue House – our wonderful B&B

As I had never been to Ireland before, I was looking forward to experiencing the hospitality for which the Irish are renowned. Peter and I headed out on our first evening and teamed up with two other marshals to check out the local hostelries after playing a round of golf. We were not to be disappointed as the local pub welcomed us with open arms and, after only a few minutes, the young landlord was asking where we were from and what had brought us to the area. Although he wasn't a golfer himself, he was fascinated by the comings and goings around the area during the build-up to the Ryder Cup Matches as the massive infrastructure rolled into town.

We became regulars at this pub and, each evening, after we had returned from The K Club, we would be greeted by the locals as 'the marshals' and quizzed on the events of the day. The regulars wanted to know what was going down at the golf event and loved hearing stories of famous names that they had heard about. We had a meal there every evening; the food was excellent, the beer was tasty, and the craic was first class. We made that pub our regular haunt each evening after our visit to the course and had many great nights there in the company of such friendly Irish people. The landlord told us that we had to get to the bar by 7:30pm on the Saturday if we wanted to eat as they were holding a music evening that night and the place was usually oversubscribed.

As luck would have it, both Peter and I had afternoon duties at The K Club on the Saturday in question, which meant we weren't able to leave as early as we wanted to get to the pub in time. Our hearts sank as we didn't get back to our B&B until just after 7:30 pm and, with lightning quick changes of clothes, we didn't make it to the pub until about 7:40pm. We had well resigned ourselves to just a pint and a packet of crisps.

As we walked through the door, the whole place was packed with wall-to-wall drinkers, and we reckoned it really would be crisps or peanuts for us. However, the landlord spotted me (sometimes being six foot four is an advantage) and waved us across to where a table was set for two with a 'Reserved for the Marshals' sign on it. Not only had the landlord saved us a table but the chef stayed on to cook us dinner! He normally had left by 7:30pm. There was no choice, it was fish and chips because that was what was being prepared! We certainly weren't going to argue with that choice, and it was one of the most enjoyable meals I have ever had, not least of all because my stomach had prepared itself for salted crisps.

Yes, the hospitality of the Irish was alive and kicking in Wicklow! Up to that point, I had always thought that Scotland was the place for hospitality, but I have to say that the Irish brought it to another level.

My application form had contained a note that I wanted to work as a scoring marshal in the same way as I had done at The Belfry in 2002 under the stewardship of John Wardle. I had seen a list of officials and I noticed that even Barry Drew hadn't been designated as Chief Marshal, so duties were likely to be quite different to what we had done at The Belfry back in 2002.

A note had been sent out by the Irish Chief Marshal, a gentleman by the name of David O'Hora and, more importantly John Wardle had not been appointed Chief

Scorer – that role was awarded to a Vincent Ferguson. I must confess that the appeal of this revised set-up troubled me slightly until I got there and found that Vincent delegated all scoring duties to John Wardle, and everything was as before. If it's not broke, don't fix it! What a relief that was because I was familiar with John's organisational abilities, and he also had Pete Houghton with him as his assistant, so the team would be familiar to me.

David O'Hora's welcome letter arrived 125 days before the Ryder Cup was to take place – it said so at the top of his letter. His letter was indeed welcome as it stated that the respective roles of all 800 marshals would be allocated to get the best possible support for this event's first visit to Ireland.

As soon as we arrived at the course, John Wardle took us to one side and explained that we would work in the same way as before; wonderful news, which was a great relief as John had established a very professional system for organising his Walking Scorers. It was great to meet several other Walking Scorers from clubs around the area and we were soon ready for briefing by the tournament director. The team spirit felt palpable, and a sense of mounting anticipation reverberated around the Marshals' Headquarters as uniforms and lunch vouchers were handed out.

At the end of the briefing by David O'Hora, we were each handed a card with our duties indicated for each of the three competition days.

My card showed:
Tuesday: Practice
Wednesday: Practice
Thursday: Training AM and Opening Ceremony PM.
Friday: AM Match No.2 and PM – Off Duty.
Saturday: AM – Off Duty and PM – Match No.7.
Sunday: Draw

Of course, Walking Scorers didn't know who they would be walking with until the Team Captains declared their pairings on the evening before the day's play. I waited with some anticipation to find out who would be playing in Match No. 2, and this was revealed as Paul Casey and Robert Karlsson v Stewart Cink and J.J. Henry. Both Karlsson and Henry were 'Rookies', having not played in the Ryder cup before. I had met Paul Casey several times at various European Tour events and briefly met Stewart Cink at St Andrews the year before. I had also walked with Robert Karlsson and Mark O'Meara at Hoylake earlier that year along with Robert's caddie – "Lordy". It must be said that any pairings of golfers at this level are going to throw up lots of excitement and high-quality golf.

The K Club course was designed by Arnold Palmer and was the brainchild of the President and Owner, Dr Michael Smurfit, who, when interviewed, confessed that he had purchased two pairs of golf shoes, both a USA Team pair in red and a European Team pair in blue. He wore one of each to show his complete neutrality during the event! Our marshal outfits were dark green with a slight plaid look; very distinctive and one that I still wear with pride to this very day.

The format for the 2006 Ryder Cup Matches was the same as that in 2002.

The European Team consisted of: **Henrik Stenson, Luke Donald, Sergio Garcia, David Howell, Colin Montgomerie, Paul Casey, Robert Karlsson, Padraig Harrington, Paul McGinley, Jose Maria Olazábal, Darren Clarke and Lee Westwood.** Their Captain was **Ian Woosnam**.

Team USA consisted of: **Tiger Woods, Phil Mickelson, Jim Furyk,** Chad Campbell, **David Toms**, Chris DiMarco, Vaughn Taylor, J.J. Henry, **Zach Johnson**, Brett Wetterich, **Stewart Cink** & Scott Verplank. Their Captain was **Tom**

Lehman. By this time, I had already met and seen the players in bold, either at a European Tour event or at The Open Championships at St Andrews and Hoylake, earlier in the year.

At the Opening Ceremony, which was a very lavish affair, the Irish Prime Minister – Mr Bertie Ahern – stated that the Ryder Cup was an excellent opportunity to put Ireland on the map as he quoted a worldwide audience of one billion people in one hundred and fifty countries plus sixty million golfers. The Ceremony was performed under a massive half-dome-shaped stage enclosure with Irish music and dancing before the appearance of the teams on the stage. I was standing to one side alongside Thomas Levet – the French golfer – and he commented on how wonderful it was to see such a magnificent spectacle. Watching the two teams walk out onto the stage was a moment of realisation that here we were on the eve of a great event. Of course, Irish players figured in the shape of Darren Clarke, Padraig Harrington, and Paul McGinley and that added a sense of identity for the European Team. Darren Clarke was one of the few players to record a round of 60 and that feat had been achieved here at The K Club.

The audience consisted of all the local dignitaries and the players' wives and girlfriends sitting in the front few rows. The terms 'Wags' had been spawned some time before by footballers' wives and girlfriends, but these women were elegantly dressed and in great supportive mood. After the speeches by Tom Lehman and Ian Woosnam, the following day's four balls were announced, and the players' names appeared on a giant display board at the back of the ceremony area. There was a great deal of chattering about the matches once the pairings had been posted. The excitement levels were ramped up to an even higher level.

Thomas Levet at the Opening Ceremony

Team USA WAGS (wives and girlfriends)

In the days before the Matches got underway, we were privileged to walk out on the course while both teams were practising, and it was wonderful to see some of the greatest players in the world laughing and joking with each other as they acquainted themselves with the golf course.

My most wonderful memory of The K Club was the sound of the crowd cheering for Darren Clarke as he stepped on to the first tee on the first day. His wife, Heather, had only recently passed away and there was some doubt about whether he would be in any state to play. However, Ian Woosnam, Europe Team Captain, had asked him if he really wanted to play (his golf was really on top form at the time). Of course, Darren agreed to play, and he had said that both Heather and his children would have wanted him to play. Who can tell what was going through his mind as he met with such a wonderful ovation. The emotion of the moment was almost too much, and I have never felt such a collective support for any player in all my days as a volunteer or spectator. The noise was deafening around the first tee area and Ivor Robson had to wait for some time before he could announce the players' names. Darren himself was clearly moved by the support he received.

Day 1 – Friday – Team Europe won two of the morning fourballs and one of the afternoon foursomes with an overnight score of 5-3. I walked with Match No.2 in the morning – Paul Casey & Robert Karlsson v Stewart Cink and J.J. Henry. It was a tight match and just about a fair result, depending on which side of the Atlantic that you resided. At least the rain stopped in time for the matches to be played but the ground was heavy in parts which made walking a gruelling and tiring operation. I bumped into Paul Casey's wife from time to time while she followed Paul. I introduced myself when I got the chance. Her name was Jocelyn – the same name as my first niece – so it stuck in my memory. She was just a part of the entourage that was to accompany play around the course. I was amazed at just how many people were 'inside the ropes' and it became quite difficult to plot my way around the place and do my scoring duties properly.

Walking from the course that evening, I bumped into Pat Jennings OBE, the Northern Ireland goalkeeper and asked him if he minded me taking a photograph of him. He was very polite and agreed to smile for the camera. He had such a distinctive hairstyle; it was easy to spot him in a crowd. I was to see him again in 2019 at Portrush – more of that later.

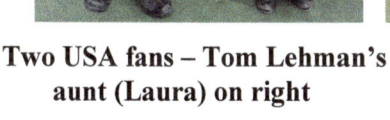

Two USA fans – Tom Lehman's aunt (Laura) on right **Tom Lehman – Team USA Captain**

I also took some photographs of some Team USA fans in Stars and Stripes outfits and when I asked one pair of lovelies where they were from, one of them said that she was Tom Lehman's aunt by the name of Laura. I couldn't believe my luck but, as I say often, if you put yourself out there, opportunities will arise for such encounters. We had a long chat and she told me a little about Tom's golfing career and how proud she was of him.

The very next day, I found myself standing right next to Tom on the first tee as I was preparing to walk the course. I nudged him and said that I had been chatting with his aunt the day before when I had taken my photograph. He asked if I was a keen photographer and I told him about my special collection which included a photo of him that he had autographed although he couldn't remember the occasion. I joked that it was disgraceful that he couldn't remember me! He said that it was nice to talk about something other than golf for five minutes.

Day 2 – Saturday – Team Europe stretched their lead to an overnight score of 10-6 and I walked with Match No.7, which was the afternoon foursomes between Paul Casey & David Howell v Steward Cink and Zach Johnson, a match which the European pairing won 5&4 with its dramatic conclusion on the 14th Tee. As I had walked with Stewart Cink the day before, I had already become friendly with his caddie who was a very chatty American and we exchanged stories on our way round in the middle of the heat of battle! Quite extraordinary really. It was my experience that caddies were generally happy to engage with anyone who was 'inside the ropes'.

Howell and Casey were 3-up as we walked along the fairway of the 13th Hole – a right to left dog-leg hole with trees on the left and a wide stream on the right, beyond which the far bank was packed with spectators standing about ten deep. Suddenly, to our left, security men appeared out of a gap in the trees with their hands inside their jackets – just like the movies! It immediately recalled a show where I had seen Eddie Izzard make fun of such positions where he would remove his hand from inside his jacket and say, "Bunch of flowers!" Where do these thoughts come from at a time like this?

Bill Clinton then appeared from the gap and the American players immediately stood to attention, giving their President a salute (I was surprised at how short he was). Although Bill Clinton wasn't President at that time, Americans always call their ex-Presidents 'Mr President'.

Forgetting myself and being caught in the moment, I said, "Hi, Bill!"

I still can't believe that I was so gauche, but Bill Clinton responded with a casual, "Hi, buddy. Having a good day?"

How I wished I could have that moment again and show a bit more respect for their President. It was one of those moments in life where I had to pinch myself to come to terms with the fact that I had just met a President of the USA. My name-dropping armoury was strengthened even further in that moment.

On the next hole, the 14th, Paul Casey holed his tee shot.

From the tee, because of the topography of the hole where the green was slightly raised, we didn't see the ball go in the hole but there was a large screen behind which showed the moment that the ball dropped. Of course, the place erupted as that meant that Europe had won the match by 4&3! I haven't been able to confirm this but one of the scorers told me that Ryder Cup convention meant that the opposing team were also awarded the same score in the event of the hole being won before they'd even hit a ball!

I asked Paul's wife is she could get Paul to sign his ball for me and she was told in no uncertain terms that the ball would remain in his possession for posterity! However, Paul did sign a ball for me, and it is now in my treasured collection of autographed golf balls – see later page with a view of some of my collection.

Newspaper photograph of Paul celebrating

Paul Casey's signed golf ball

Look out for some trivia quiz which poses the question, 'Name a time when a golfer recorded a hole-in-one without hitting a ball'?

Paul's hole-in-one was only the sixth in Ryder Cup Matches history. Previous aces had been scored by Peter Butler, Sir Nick Faldo, Costantino Rocca, Howard Clark and now Paul Casey was to join this illustrious select group. Oddly enough, American Scott Verplank scored an ace the very next day at the same hole! So, there was a sequence of names to be memorised and recalled at some future discussion about holes-in-one! It brought memories flooding back of my one and only hole-in-one at Henbury Golf Club in 2002 when my bar bill was £67.78. It was a tradition for anyone holing in one to buy everyone in the clubhouse a drink and I wondered how much Paul Casey would have to pay later that day! Undoubtedly, he would have insurance against such an event.

After that round, I was just de-briefing the scoreboard carrier when I was approached by two elderly gentlemen who introduced themselves. "We're David and Paul's dads!" and they explained that they had walked all the way round behind us watching proudly as their sons played their hearts out.

David's father said, "We have been watching you closely and we both admired how you shepherded that young scoreboard carrier round the course. You always took time to make sure he was standing in the right position and kept him right by your side all the time. Well done, you!" And they shook my hand. I later contacted David Howell to obtain his approval to include this story about his dad and found out, to my sorrow that he (Raymond) had sadly passed away a few years ago. I gave David my condolences, but he was pleased to hear that his father had been so thoughtful.

I was overwhelmed by this and felt a warm glow inside as I always treated the board carriers with the greatest respect, most of whom were keen young golfers with handicaps in single figures. I had noticed other scorers who totally ignored their board carriers in their efforts to either get a better view or simply view them as dogsbodies.

As Walking Scorers, there is an air of competitiveness about which scorer is walking with the match where the winning putt is holed. Before the final round, the mood in the camp was that 'Fowler' would undoubtedly get it. I'm not quite sure where that thought came from as I hadn't been with Paul McGinley when he holed the winning putt in 2002. Nevertheless, I conveyed to my friends that it was bound to be me!

Day 3 – Sunday – Team Europe won eight of the twelve singles matches with a final score of 18½ to 9½, an emphatic win indeed and their third in succession. I walked with Match No.8, which was between Henrik Stenson and

Vaughn Taylor with Stenson holing the putt that secured the win at the 15th Hole. It was a tight match and at one point, Henrik went 1-down so my thoughts of securing the winning putt were looking slim at that point in the round.

Standing on the fairway of the 15th Hole, Sandy Lyle – one of Ian Woosnam's vice captains – stood next to me and advised me that Luke Donald was about to putt for the draw in his singles match, which would ensure that Europe at least retained the Ryder Cup. In fact, we heard the cheer as Luke's putt dropped. Henrik then steadied himself and sank his fifteen-foot putt, which meant that Europe had indeed won the Ryder Cup outright.

Television coverage of that moment shows me walking on to the green to congratulate Henrik. Luckily, there was no Chief Marshal around to reprimand me for walking on the hallowed turf as everyone in sight was doing so as well. Oops – 'no partisan behaviour' rang in my ears, so apologies to any Americans reading this.

The scenes around Darren Clarke's win over Zach Johnson were phenomenal with Darren finally succumbing to the pent-up emotions that he had tried so hard to suppress earlier in the matches. I saw a softer side to Tiger Woods that afternoon as he shared a quiet moment with Darren who, by that stage, was openly weeping tears of joy and sadness combined. How wonderful to see a world-class sportsman display such raw emotion, reminiscent of the scenes at Hoylake earlier in the year when Tiger won only months after his beloved father had passed away.

After Europe had already won, Paul McGinley conceded a 25-foot putt to J.J. Henry on the 18th Hole, thereby halving their match. If Henry had putted and missed, Europe's final total would have been a record victory over the Americans. McGinley conceded the putt because an almost-naked spectator ran across the green and jumped into the lake as Henry was about to putt. This was not shown on television and McGinley's action has been described as an example of the "sportsmanship that has come to signify the Ryder Cup Matches".

This was reminiscent of Jack Nicklaus conceding a two-foot putt to Tony Jacklin in 1969 at Royal Birkdale (which, had he missed, Team USA would have won the Cup) when Jack Nicklaus said, "I don't think you would have missed it, but in these circumstances, I wasn't going to give you the chance, either!"

I had read somewhere that Jack's action was not appreciated by all of Team USA, particularly Captain Sam Snead who apparently said, "We went over there to win, not to be good ol' boys!" In 1999, the late Payne Stewart conceded his singles match to Colin Montgomerie as a response to the abuse that Colin had received throughout the match – an act that signalled the need for both teams to work hard to restore the integrity of golf at The Belfry in 2002. Behaviour at the Ryder Cup Matches tends to stray towards football-style tribalism, and it is incumbent on all spectators to keep their enthusiasm within the bounds of the great game's history.

Photograph of the Scorers with John Wardle (kneeling at the front of the group) and Peter Houghton (back row)

Scorers relaxing after the Ryder Cup was won by Europe

Celebrations with spectators

When Peter and I returned home, we spent many hours reminiscing about the wonderful event that we had just experienced.

Shortly after returning from Ireland, and sporting my tartan Ryder Cup jacket, I headed for Scotland to play golf with my architect buddies with whom I had played golf since studying architecture at Edinburgh College of Art in the 1960s. We have stayed close friends ever since and meet every five years since to celebrate an enduring friendship under the banner of a curious title known as "Bimbo Plenderleith"! Enough to say that Bimbo was coined by a fellow student back in 1967 when he handed in bogus design studies under that fictional name! In the photographs are Alex Keighren, Merv Archibald, Alan Clyde (standing in for Alex in the right-hand photo), Mike Lamont and me. The photographs were taken at West Lothian Golf Club which has fabulous views of no less than five counties.

Alex, Merv, Mike and Doug

Doug with Merv, Alan and Mike at West Lothian GC

CHAPTER 9 (2007)
THE WALES OPEN

In 2007, I moved out of Bristol to live in Clevedon where I joined a wonderful small golf club at Tickenham. There I met a lovely bunch of people who had the love of golf as the glue which bound them all together. The captain of the club was one Stewart Galway who, although born in England, was Scottish through parenthood and it was in his soul. Together with Andrew Camper, Stewart and I introduced a competition which was known as The Auchentoshan Cup.

Some members had overheard me chatting to a fellow member from Inverurie, Charlie McWilliam, when we were discussing Auchentoshan whisky. The members assumed that were we swearing at each other in some Gaelic tongue! I sponsored the Auchentoshan Cup and, after an approach to the distillery, their marketing manager sent us a generous donation of glasses and vouchers together with a few other branded items. I called in to the distillery, near Clydebank, on my way north soon after and managed to negotiate for a bobble hat to present to each of the entrants who participated in the first competition. The cup is now played for annually on the last Saturday before Christmas.

Left to right: Andrew Camper, Charlie Camper, Stewart Galway, Doug, Charlie McWilliam and Doug Garrett

In the above photograph, we were all proudly wearing our Auchentoshan bobble hats. Charlie Camper was the winner of the inaugural Auchentoshan Cup. My mixed foursomes playing partner, Jayne Baker, introduced me to her mother, Pam, one day and I soon established that she had a love of the Auchentoshan amber nectar too. Buying a Christmas present for Pam was easy after that declaration!

Members of Tickenham GC celebrating after the cup presentation ceremony

I was promoted to Senior Marshal for The Wales Open this year, because of John Wardle's recommendation to Barry Drew. It was John's way of rewarding me for my sterling performance at the other events and I have to say it was a privilege as well as an honour. Apart from the prestigious armband, Senior Marshals were also invited to a golfing event beforehand where much of the pre-planning took place. This felt like a real step up and I repaid the trust in me by undertaking a complete review of the scoring system, which John implemented immediately. I had spent hours writing the new handbook ensuring that scorers were made aware of all the duties that had to be performed with reference to their working closely with scoreboard carriers.

It was one of my real pleasures in the game when I persuaded the Senior Scoring Marshal at The Wales Open that my job would be to introduce the Walking Scorer and the Scoreboard Carrier to the players and Ivor Robson before they set off on their round. Ivor was always the gentleman, taking time to speak to the scorers and scoreboard carriers as they were usually young golfers who were thrilled to be on the big stage at golfing tournaments. The players also seemed to like this procedure because they at least know the names of the volunteers who would be walking with them out on the course.

One of the benefits of becoming a Senior Marshal was that I had access to a buggy! Getting around the Wentwood Hills course was not easy with the different levels to negotiate on foot. I had lots of comments from fellow marshals when they saw me swanning about on my buggy. On the Pro-Am day I passed the first tee where I spotted a couple of outstandingly gorgeous girls – I thought they were models and most of the marshals were 'ogling' them as I turned up. Never one to miss an opportunity, I asked them if they would like a lift to the lower part of the course; after all, their high heels were hardly appropriate footwear for getting around a golf course! The pair of them – a blonde and a brunette – agreed readily and packed themselves into the buggy alongside me. The buggy was made for two and it was a tight squeeze for the three of us but someone has to do it!

Driving around the course with my gorgeous cargo, I was clearly the envy of all the other marshals who, to a man, were making lewd comments as I passed them. When I reached the feeding station at the lower part of the course, I decided it would be a great idea to be photographed with these beauties on my buggy. In the middle of this impromptu photo shoot, which proved that they really were models, Alan and Marion Gray walked past and said loudly, "Fowler, what on earth are you up to?!"

Alan and Marion were golfing friends who organised golf days for a group of co-workers within Lloyds Bank at the time. They looked on in disbelief as I posed for photographs with these two beauties.

Doug with two beauties on board

The girls pose after their trip on my buggy

I took the girls back up to where I had picked them up and they were grateful for my taxi services, each planting a big smacker of a kiss on my cheek before staggering off to the hospitality tent.

Later that day, Barry Drew called me to one side, as he had obviously heard about my exploits with the buggy and said firmly, "The giving of lifts in buggies to tarts is purely the prerogative of the Chief Marshal!"

It was his way of rebuking me for what I had done. He also pointed out that the buggies were designed for only two persons on the front, muttering something along the lines of, "You lucky bugger!" Anyway, I took this as a final warning and admired his way of telling me off gently.

I saw Barry again about half an hour later with his wife, Mavis, on the buggy and, while I thought it would be funny to refer to his warning, I decided that discretion was the better part of valour!

CHAPTER 10 (2008)
THE WALES OPEN & THE BRITISH MASTERS

The 2008 Wales Open was to be my last and, indeed, the end of my relationship with Barry and Mavis Drew. It was all down to an unfortunate set of circumstances and misunderstandings – don't all relationships end that way?

It all started to unravel when Barry Drew approached me, saying that there were too many Senior Marshals on the scoring team (I think there were two of us) and, if I wanted to remain as a Senior Marshal, I would have to work with the marshals who operated around the course generally. I so enjoyed my scoring role that I decided to forego my senior status on the basis that I would work for John Wardle on his scorers' team thereafter. After all, that was where all my experience had been gained over the previous eight years.

I had carried out my Walking Scorer's duties on the Friday and been advised that I didn't need to turn up so early the following day as my scoring allocation would be reserved for me. I had Darren Hayes – a fellow marshal – staying at my home in Bristol and we welcomed this change in plan whereby we didn't need to get up early and leave for the course at some ungodly early hour. We had a leisurely breakfast before heading out and, apart from the slightly heavier traffic, the journey over the Severn Bridge was quite easy at that time of day.

When we arrived at Marshals' HQ, we had to join the queue checking in because Mavis had to tick us off her list and allocate lunch vouchers, etc. When I got to the front of the queue, Mavis said, "Marshalling," and asked me to report to the Senior Marshal for a zone of the course. When I queried why I wasn't down for scoring, Mavis simply said that all those jobs had been filled! As I looked around, I could see some young marshals, with no scoring experience whatsoever, preparing to go out on to the course. I couldn't understand this change of plan, particularly as the Saturday usually involved more intense pressure as the crowds of spectators almost doubled.

I was so annoyed that I said I didn't want to simply be a marshal as my scoring competencies were never in question so why use younger marshals with no experience whatsoever in the 'battlefield', that is competition days at the weekend? So, I headed off to leave and Barry Drew followed me saying that I shouldn't be such a 'prima donna' and that I should just do as I was told. I explained to him that, had I known that the allocation of scoring duties was to be so arbitrarily handed out, I would have arrived at my normal time to ensure that I was allocated to John Wardle. I was so angry that I just walked off the course and headed for home with Darren by my side – he was happy to accompany me home where he collected his stuff and headed back to Droitwich where he lived.

I have to say that Darren's involvement in the overall situation left me doubly angry as he returned to the course alone the following day and was appointed Senior Marshal to fill the place that I had vacated – at least, that was what appeared to happen.

I had a harsh exchange of email messages with Barry Drew, whereby we both exchanged views freely, but he eventually offered me the hand of friendship by saying that I could still be part of the team at the 2010 Ryder Cup, which would be staged at Celtic Manor. However, I stubbornly stuck to my guns and decided to cut my ties with the European Tour and concentrate only on working at The Open Championship thereafter – a decision I was not to regret, particularly as the 2010 Ryder Cup Matches were such a washout with torrential rain delaying completion of the competition until the Monday after the event.

It would be remiss of me not to clarify that Barry and I then exchanged friendly letters where we agreed to let bygones be bygones, but I never saw Barry or Mavis ever again. Nevertheless, I owed them both a huge vote of thanks for the good times that I had enjoyed under their command before it all unravelled unexpectedly.

I withdrew my application for The British Masters that year and it was two years later before I returned to my scoring duties at The Open. At this point, I need to clarify that I applied to work at each Open Championship thereafter but, due to the high demand for such placements, I wasn't guaranteed acceptance every year.

After leaving the service of Barry and Mavis, I read this article in a Reuters publication about their involvement at The Ryder Cup in 2010:

"Starting on Friday, the Drews are on site at 5am every day coordinating a military-like exercise to organise the 1,300 volunteer marshals who have descended on the Usk Valley. From a small white portacabin surrounded by a variety of golf buggies, the English couple begin their day at the crack of dawn and are still working long after the fans have gone home. But with more than 50 years' experience of marshalling between them, the Drews operate a well-oiled machine and do not stand for any nonsense."

"We had more than 2,000 applications from all over the world but 80 percent of the marshals we have used have experience at previous Ryder Cups," Mavis, codename MAM (Marshalls Administration Manager) told Reuters on Tuesday as their army of blue-jacketed helpers went to work. "I think they're frightened of me! But seriously, they are like a huge family."

"The Drews first marshalled at the Ryder Cup at the Belfry in 1993 and since then it has become a passion. This is their eighth Ryder Cup, and they have an in-depth knowledge of Celtic Manor having organised the marshals at the Wales Open since 2002."

"The Wales Open can't compare to this though," Mavis said. "The infrastructure is enormous. Nothing comes close. Remember, we're also volunteers. But I love it, I love people."

My memory fails me when I try to recall what happened at The British Masters that year as, although it was in my schedule to attend, my falling out with the Drews probably meant that I withdrew. Unusually, I can find no record of that event in my files. I know that the event had moved to The Belfry but that's as far as it goes – my brain draws a blank. In any event, 2008 was to mark the end of my volunteering with the European Tour – an eight-year stretch that contained so many golden moments that I will never forget. Nevertheless, I was determined to throw all my effort into making the most of my scoring jobs at The Open, a decision that I have never regretted.

CHAPTER 11 (2010)
THE OPEN (ST ANDREWS)

Having waved goodbye to the European Tour, my volunteering journey now consisted of working at The Open Championship, which was held every five years at St Andrews – 2000, 2005, 2010, 2015 and so on, only for the pattern to be disrupted by the pandemic in 2020, which resulted in the 150th staging of the championship being held at St Andrews in 2022. The Ryder Cup Matches were also cancelled in 2020, thereby reverting to being held on odd-numbered years as they had since its inception in 1927 – other than the intervention of World War 2.

At The Open Championship, the training session was quite an experience as there were quite a few changes to the handheld devices and the functions that had been introduced in the intervening period since I'd worked at Hoylake in 2006.

In addition to the now regular use of the paper recording sheets, as shown above, I was going to need my wits about me because, as Ryan the presenter who had replaced Ralus, mentioned, there was a hunger for even more information from Walking Scorers. The paper sheets were used for basic information, i.e., the number of shots taken by each player at each hole. The lower section showed the player's score against par with either +3 or -4 showing after each hole and this had to correspond with the information displayed on the board carried by the scoreboard carrier.

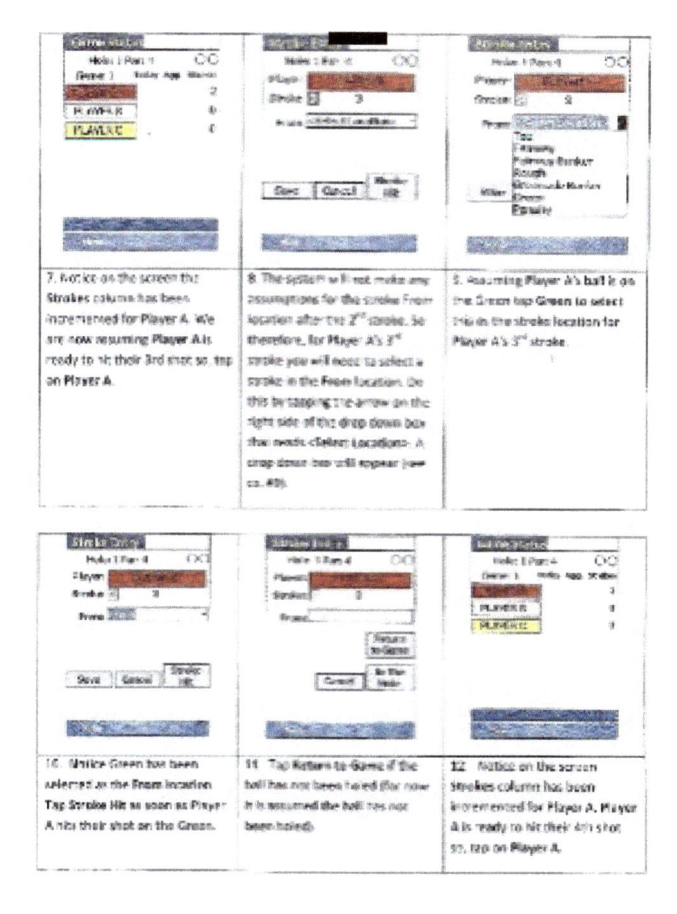

Technical instructions for Walking Scorers

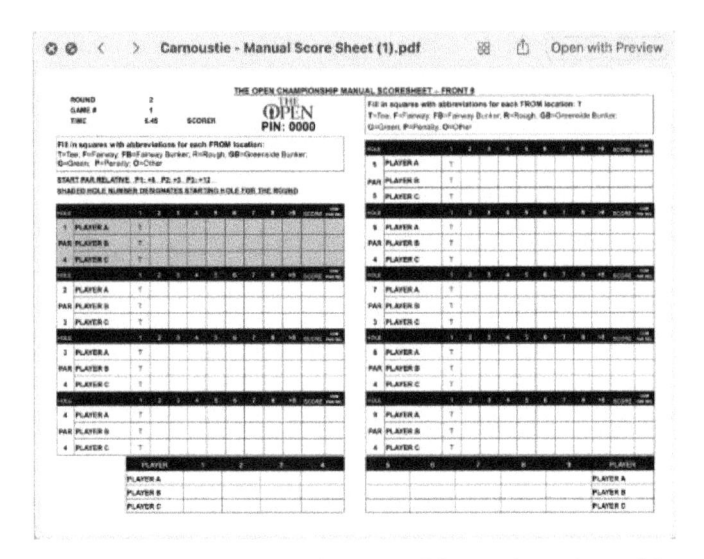

Typical manual score sheet used in conjunction with handheld computer

When out on the course, I always double-checked each player's score with the Match Referee, who always carried a little black book although they had no scoring responsibilities. It was also quite sensible to make this check after a ruling or a player playing a provisional ball or the like. A bit like 'measure twice, cut once' – one couldn't be too careful at this job. The paper form was always considered as 'back-up' and if we didn't have a chance to complete it, it wasn't too much of a problem. Nevertheless, like all other areas of my job as a Walking Scorer, I took my responsibilities seriously and only once failed to complete the form, mainly because it had disintegrated in the wet conditions towards the end of a round.

During the training session, I learned that more facilities were built into the software, and it would be possible to trace a player's progress from tee to green via fairway bunkers, rough, greenside bunkers and out-of-bounds. In addition, information about the ball's position on the green was a new feature that required our assessment of the length of putt.

All this information was for television coverage solely and would be used as an aide for commentators while describing action out on the course. I don't know if viewers of golf on their televisions realise the infrastructure which enables the commentators to say, "He's now playing his third shot," and so on. The service relies heavily on the ability of the Walking Scorers to convey the right information in a very timely manner as it was being broadcast in real time. There was always a sense of urgency around any situation where our scoring information differed with that shown on TV.

In terms of efficient management of scoring information, the R&A left nothing to chance, and we even had a chart which showed exactly where we should stand – on every hole – both at the tee and by the green so that a fast exit could be made to the next tee. These arrangements were made in advance because of the lack of space on some of the championship tees and, at times, the Walking Scorer had to go there along with the Scoreboard Carriers and Bunker Rakers staying some way away. I always looked upon the trio as a small team and had a briefing before we set off to ensure that we acted together. For example, it was vital for the Scoreboard Carriers to be ready to update their scores before players teed off at the next tee. The Bunker Rakers sometimes went for several holes without having to restore a bunker to its pristine state but, on one or two occasions, their fairly relaxed round would spring into frantic activity if two separate players had to play out of greenside bunkers on opposite sides of the green!

Sometimes I had to hold back some enthusiastic Scoreboard Carrier from making changes while a player was about to putt as absolute silence was required. Also, the scoreboards could weigh heavily on some of these youngsters so I would always suggest that they turn the board upside down while they were standing still as all spectators' eyes would be on the action in front of them. In high winds also, I suggested that they hold their boards upside down because spectators were generally battling against the elements themselves. It was always a matter of judgment, but it was important to me to be always professional and efficient while on the course.

The basic scoring record, relayed directly from our handheld devices, would also be displayed back at the R&A's Recorder's Office where the players could see this information (displayed on a long TV monitor which was positioned on the wall above the officials so that the players could see their scores directly) while checking their scorecards before signing off their rounds; quite a responsibility if ever to be called into use should there be a dispute, but I never once had my information queried, thank goodness!

I recall one heart-stopping moment when Paul Casey turned to me and said that he was surprised that I had shown his second shot, on a Par 3 hole, being hit from the rough whereas he recalled that his tee shot stopped just short of the green. I explained that our devices didn't have a facility to record fairway on a Par 3 – it was either 'on the green' or 'in the rough'.

"Just wondered," he said as he turned back to sign his card.

My breathing relaxed and I managed to make it to the end of the session without further questions.

After the players completed their card signing, an R&A official would then take the Walking Scorer through to an outer office where the score entries were double-checked to ensure that all scores were accurately recorded before they were committed to the record book. I had a 100% record of providing accurate information; after all, anything less would have let the side down and, as volunteers, we were proud of our contribution to the smooth running of this famous event.

In the training notes, the latest diagrams showing the display screen on the handheld device, the green now showed concentric circles around the pin position which would help us with our estimate of the putt length. When clicking the button marked 'In the Hole' one had to be careful that the player didn't miss a tap-in putt as this would throw the scoring out at that moment. It didn't pay to be 'trigger happy' but I did develop a technique of preparing the button just to be pressed as soon as I saw the ball disappear into the bottom of the cup. Back at Control, the organisers didn't like it if the scores were delayed, particularly if television commentators were quoting scores that we hadn't yet confirmed.

We ran through quite a few scenarios, and I needed to concentrate hard with my new spectacles that had been prescribed recently. Years of architectural drawings with fine pens had taken their toll on my 60-year-old eyes. To make matters worse, weather conditions deteriorated the following day to the extent that the R&A limited practice to just the first four outward and return holes, i.e., the first to the fourth followed by the fifteenth to the eighteenth. Quite a few scorers gave the on-course training a miss, but I really had to test my eyesight in the driving rain because I just had to see the small screen clearly.

Ralus and Ryan, our trainers, had prepared for the eventuality by handing out clear plastic bags which would contain not only the handheld device but also the clipboard with the paper score sheet. It may have seemed a great idea, but the reality was that the interior of the plastic misted up with condensation and made reading the information almost impossible. The use of an umbrella was out of the question as we would have literally needed two sets of hands to hold the clipboard, the handheld device, the radio, and the umbrella itself. The arrival of stiff winds of over forty miles an hour didn't help the situation.

Nevertheless, a hardy group of about seven scorers decided to give it a go and we set off down the first fairway into the teeth of a stiff wind blowing in off the sea from the right. Panic set in as my glasses started to attract droplets of water and my vision of the screen became blurred! Determination to overcome this issue drove me on and I adjusted my golf cap so that the brim offered some protection to my spectacles, which had to be perched on the end of my nose as I didn't need them for long-distance sight. I can remember the feelings of concern that I was going to let the side down if I couldn't overcome these conditions. The show must go on – and I persevered with the group, making it all the way down to the second hole before abandoning the session, as did most of the players who had ventured out that morning.

A friendly marshal took a photograph of our bedraggled party by the first tee as we made our way back to Scorer's Headquarters, dripping wet with our equipment sealed in the plastic bags. I wasn't the only one who expressed concern about the conditions and suggesting that we needed to abandon the paper score sheets as these had been reduced to soaking rags which were falling apart.

A soaked Doug outside the R&A!

Uniforms drying in readiness for next day's play

Although they were essential back-up, it just wouldn't be possible to open and close the plastic bags in the wind without destroying the paper and the information contained therein. Ever the optimist, Ralus declared that he had obtained waterproof paper which would help overcome the problem although I doubted that the standard pencil would work with that combination, as proved to be the case. Thankfully, the weather abated, and the competition days were somewhat milder, albeit play was halted for over an hour on the Friday afternoon due to the high winds.

During one of my break periods, I wandered over to the Tented Village for a coffee before searching for a seat somewhere. I found a space at a table where about eight or nine spectators were indulging in some food and drink. I got chatting to them, asking where they were from, and it transpired this was a first for the group, who had just arrived in Scotland from the USA, and they were renting a cottage in Anstruther. Dressed in waterproofs, the group looked like they had been on the course in the worst of the weather.

One woman in the group intrigued me as she had a camera round her neck housed in a waterproof plastic container protecting the lens from the wet. On closer inspection, as I asked her to show me her camera kit, I noticed that it was the same underwater protection that I had purchased for my digital camera a few years beforehand when I was trying out scuba diving in Bristol. This container – an ingenious device with rubber seals and cunning levers to connect the controls to the camera body – was designed to operate to a depth of thirty metres where the water pressure would be four-bar or fifty-eight pounds per square inch! She said that she had heard that it got wet in Scotland.

When I returned to my accommodation, everything had to be dried, including my golf shoes, which needed stuffing with paper to absorb the dampness inside. My hostess, Moira, did a sterling job of cleaning up my clothes and restoring my equilibrium in readiness for another session in the morning. I mentioned this in my account of the 2005 Championship.

On the Thursday, I decided to watch some golf while I was on a rest period, and I decided to take a seat in the stand adjacent to the second tee where there was also a good view back up the first fairway and the first green. One of the lovely features of The Open is the provision of free seating in the many stands around the course, the only downside being that one had to queue for a seat, and this sometimes involved quite a long wait. I entered the stand and noticed a space at the top of the steps where a couple of seats had good space in front for long-legged individuals like me.

When I took my seat, I suddenly realised that I was sitting right next to Sir Clive Woodward, Coach of the England Team that had won the Rugby World Cup back in 2003 in Australia. I immediately put his mind at rest by explaining that I knew who he was, congratulated him on his success and promised not to bother him anymore. Little did he know how much of a challenge that was for me!

Neither of us had an order of play on us and he nudged me shortly thereafter asking me if I knew who was in the next group walking down the first fairway. In the distance, I was able to identify the unmistakeable gait of Sir Nick Faldo walking down the left-hand side of the fairway. Sir Clive expressed his surprise that I could tell from that distance, while the players were effectively in silhouette, so I explained my involvement in scoring at these events and I had a lot of experience of walking with most of the top players. He proceeded to quiz me when each group appeared and I'm proud to say that I had 100% correct identification of the players approaching the first green. Mind you, it was easy when John Daly appeared as I had walked with him on one of the practice days.

When he got up to leave, Sir Clive thanked me for my time, and I glowed with pride knowing that I would have another tale to tell in my sequence of bumping into famous people! We shook hands and said goodbye – it was a wonderful moment.

On the second day, I was down to score for the three-ball that included Tiger Woods and, while most scorers would give their eye teeth to walk with this giant of the game, having had such an unfortunate experience at the Ryder Cup Matches in 2002, I wasn't looking forward to the experience. While waiting to receive my computer and radio in the Scoring Headquarters, a young scorer said how lucky I was to be walking with Tiger. I told him that if he wanted to, I would swap with him and take the next group. Much to the lad's amazement, the Chief Scorer agreed to this, and the young man was 'happy as Larry' as a result. There can't be many golfing fans who would spurn the chance to walk with Tiger, but I had no interest in the inevitable circus that followed him around the course. In addition, my bad experiences at The Belfry and Hoylake had soured my appreciation of this great golfer.

My swapped group turned out to be a real pleasure as it included Miguel Angel Jiménez and he was one of the most loved golfers of his time. Always dressed immaculately, he had the walk of a very confident player. I noticed that spectators were always clapping him just for being there, a popular man and great company. His practice swing was something to behold as it bore little resemblance to his actual swing. Peter Alliss once did a running commentary of his warm-up routine on the driving range – a very funny moment in golf.

Regarding popular golfers, I always found Stephen Gallacher, nephew of former Ryder Cup captain Bernard Gallacher, to be an absolute gentleman. He always greeted me with a warm smile and handshake. I think being a fellow

Scot strengthened my liking of him. I was thrilled when he was selected to play for Team Europe in the Ryder Cup Matches at Gleneagles in 2014 – a very popular and deserved selection.

Stephen Gallacher's autograph   **His uncle, Bernard Gallacher**

On the final day, although I was down as a reserve, the Chief Scorer asked if I would go out with a 'singleton' who would be first off due to an odd number of players making the cut. A singleton – playing on his own – would normally be accompanied by a local professional as a courtesy, and to mark his card, but no one was available to play on this Sunday. The R&A would be sending out a match referee, but we required a scorer to carry out the normal scoring duties.

I agreed and walked with an American, Tom Pernice Jnr, who managed his way around the course in just under three hours. Given that slow play in The Open Championship often involves rounds of over five hours, it was a pleasure to watch a game that was played so relatively quickly. Although I felt that Tom was at a disadvantage because he wouldn't have another player's ball to watch on the greens, it didn't inhibit him one bit as he moved up the leader board, ending up tied sixtieth out of a field of seventy-seven players, an improvement of six strokes.

After his round was completed, Tom was very grateful for my company and gave me a signed golf ball as thanks for my support. Although I had intended to remain at the course for the rest of the day, the excitement waned as Louis Oosthuizen was the runaway winner with a score of sixteen under, a good seven shots ahead of Lee Westwood. At the point when he had a ten-shot lead, I left the course early to avoid the heavy traffic that usually happens after the championship. Indeed, I was back at Moira's in time to watch the last few holes on television and the presentation ceremony thereafter.

CHAPTER 12 (2011)
THE OPEN (ROYAL ST GEORGE'S)

My acceptance letter for volunteering at Royal St George's arrived in early April. The Chief Scorer at this event was to be Remony Millwater – a fabulous name that I'll never forget. The letter enclosed another letter, signed by Robin Bell – Assistant Director of Championships at the R&A – which allowed us access to free parking at a reserved car park together with admission to the course before our security passes were handed out at the training session.

Security passes

A new requirement that had been introduced in 2010 was the need for a passport-style photograph for incorporation into the security pass that was to be issued for access to the course and, once more, polo shirts would be issued along with hats and waterproof jackets. So, the uniform situation had been upgraded from the previous year and we were simply advised that we should wear navy trousers or shorts along with golf shoes.

I didn't have much luck with accommodation when I returned to Sandwich in 2011 as I had lost the contact details for the couple I'd stayed with beforehand, and I thought I would try the same approach as had worked so well for me at Hoylake in 2006 when I stayed with the Bench-Capons.

I decided to ring one or two churches in Sandwich; there were only three in Sandwich, but I got through to one straight away. When I explained what I wanted to the woman who answered the phone, she explained that the church had closed and been converted to a community centre. However, when I told her how much I was prepared to pay she said, "You could always come and stay with me."

I thought that this was a real turn-up for the books, but as I was enquiring about the room she was offering, my heart sank when she asked if I liked dogs. I don't dislike dogs, it's just that I wouldn't have one by choice and I really don't like them around inside anyone's house. With a sense of foreboding, I felt my heart sink when she said that she looked after dogs and had kennels in the rear garden. Thinking that I wouldn't be bothered by 'external dogs', to my horror, when I arrived at her house, I discovered that she was a dog minder and her capacious hallway had about eight or nine large sleeping beds for an assortment of dogs. The smell was awful, but I thought this was the price I must pay for accommodation at a reasonable rate.

My room wasn't ensuite, so I left my toiletries bag on a shelf in the bathroom after I settled in on my first night. When I returned to the house after my first day at the golf course, my toiletries had been returned to my room and the woman explained that it was 'their bathroom' too! Sharing a bathroom hadn't been part of the deal, so when I was heading out on the second morning, stepping in a pile of dog poo in the hall sealed it for me – I could take this no more and decided to move out. I asked the Chief Scorer to ask all the locals if anyone knew of any place that I could bed down but, drawing a blank on that front, I decided that I couldn't stay another night in the 'doghouse' and left after play on the Saturday. It was an experience that I would never forget!

When I arrived at the course on my first day there, I was taken with all the tributes that had been posted in tribute to the late Seve Ballesteros who had passed away a few months earlier. Everyone I saw was showing emotion at his sad passing – it was a collective demonstration of raw emotion as he was loved by all golf fans.

Conditions at the course were criticised by players such as Paul Lawrie, not usually one to complain as he was brought up in my native Scotland, who complained that the notorious fourth hole was almost unplayable. He said that only five or six players could reach the fairway and that the conditions were brutal. I can sympathise with that as we all got soaked before we went out on the course. I recall watching Tiger Woods teeing off and losing his ball on the course as both he, his caddie and marshals failed to find his ball within the given time limit. Tiger said, "It's the toughest I've ever played in, even worse than Carnoustie in 1999. I had to put on another waterproof jacket. The first one was soaked through."

Doug with Hazel Irvine **Hazel Irvine at The Belfry**

Phil Parkin and Doug

On Day 1, the honour of teeing off first had been given to Jerry Kelly, who had the dubious record of having taken eleven shots at the first hole the last time he played there. He did his best not to repeat that score and I think he bogied the hole (one over par).

On Day 2, I had the pleasure of walking with Billy Horschel, and it really was gratifying to be in his company. He didn't make the cut, but he was a lovely player to watch, and it was one of those outings that seemed to pass quickly without incident. Billy signed a ball for me with his trademark autograph 'Billy Ho'.

When our group was out on the course, I noticed that in one corner adjoining properties generally had high hedges to afford the residents privacy and protection from errant golf shots. One such property caught my attention as the owners had constructed a hefty scaffold arrangement together with a sizeable deck which housed about ten or twenty seats, tables etc. There was a group of spectators enjoying a great view of the green and, to be fair, there was no rowdy behaviour from that quarter. I wondered if the occupants of that private viewing platform had been charged for the privilege. No others seemed to have followed their lead in that respect.

On Day 4, I was lucky enough to be in the vicinity of the R&A Official Office by the 18th green when Rickie Fowler was being interviewed by the press. I waited around and, when he was free, I asked if he would kindly sign a shirt that I had in my bag. As the XXL sizes were made in Taiwan for smaller people than me, the kit that I had been given would only fit someone of my grandson's age and build. As my namesake, Rickie, was happy to autograph his name across the front of this white golfing shirt – "To Ben, best wishes, Rickie Fowler" in orange-coloured felt tip. On the final day of a tournament, Rickie always wears orange in honour of Oklahoma State University which he attended after leaving school. Grandson Ben now has that signed shirt pinned to his bedroom wall.

Some autograph hunters that I met over the years tended to be more aggressive than me in their approach to players, not an approach that ever endeared them to the players, who understandably would often shun the serious autograph hunter in favour of some young child who at times didn't know who was signing their scrap of paper! However, one friendly group I met at Royal St George's were more relaxed and, if they got a signature that was great, if not, there would be another player coming along in a moment.

One of their number was a tall lad and I got chatting to him several times over the three days of practice. He showed me a concertina-style plastic folder that was packed with top quality photographs of all the current players. His collection was in alphabetical order, so he was able to quickly dive into the file when a player was approaching. I noticed that players would often stop and look closely at these pristine photographs and decline to sign as they knew that the autographed item would then appear on eBay shortly thereafter. On the final practice day, this lad said that he was fed up with standing for hours waiting for players to come along and, without hesitation, he handed me his photograph collection! I asked if he wanted money, but he declined. I still have that pile of fifty or sixty top quality photographs in my memorabilia box.

I always purchased a programme for The Open in which players were featured with lovely glossy photographs. It was always a nightmare trying to find the appropriate page when a player approached so one evening, back at the B&B, I prepared an alphabetical list of the players' names along with the page number that featured them. I thought that this was such a good idea that I wrote to the R&A suggesting that such a page could be inserted in the programme, but I never had a reply! Perhaps it was just too much trouble for someone to make the cross references. Given the meticulous manner in which The Open was masterminded, I thought it was a notable omission and still do.

As I explained earlier, I have never been interested in obtaining autographs for pecuniary purposes. My photograph collection consisted of images that were a moment in time, frozen in the image where the player looked straight at my camera and smiled. Getting their signature on a printed copy of that image gave me a unique collection that only has value to me as each image is a memory of the time that I asked the player to stop for a photograph. I always asked politely, and I recall Gary Player's comment when he agreed to pose for me at Royal St George's in 2003 – he said, "As the gentleman asked politely, I'll let him take the photograph."

In my memorabilia collection, I have built up quite a collection of signed golf balls as most players would sign brand new golf balls and give them to the Walking Scorers as a 'thank you gesture' at the end of the round. Sometimes the players would stop and sign balls for the Scoreboard Carrier and Bunker Raker. Many is the time that I would have to seek out the 'team' as the players would often sit and sign the balls after handing in their scorecard. On several occasions, if I was just given one such signed ball, I would give it to the young lad or lass who had carried the scoreboard.

Some of my collection of autographed golf balls, given to me by players as a thank you for scoring their match

As previously mentioned, probably my most prized signed golf ball is the one given to me by Mark O'Meara in 2006 at Hoylake and that is because of the circumstances around his handing me the gift. It was such an honour to be given a signed golf ball by a previous Open Champion but more so because of the way he presented it to me – a moment that is etched in my memory banks. It is a Titleist (2) ProV1 392 – I have it in my hand as I write this section. The ball that Paul Lawrie, again a previous Open Champion, gave me at Royal Troon simply has his logo on it – PL – and I can't remember why he didn't sign it. Steve Stricker's ball came to the top of the pile when the Ryder Cup Matches were played in 2020. Robert Karlsson's ball is another reminder of that morning when I walked with Mark O'Meara and Robert at Hoylake.

While walking around the course on one of my rest days, I stopped near the BBC Centre and wrote a note to Peter Alliss – in SUPER LARGE PRINT so that it would catch his eye – to tell him that it was my grandson's birthday, and I would be thrilled if he could mention that fact during one of his transmissions. Matthew, my daughter's oldest offspring, has his birthday in the middle of July and I usually missed it because it fell right in the middle of the week of The Open Championship. Peter Alliss, being the gentleman he was, read out my card and wished Matthew a very happy birthday. As I was working that afternoon, I didn't see the broadcast myself, but my sister-in-law said that she heard my name and her ears pricked up. I was so thrilled when I watched it on catch-up! It was typical of Peter that he took time out to be so generous with his time on air.

In 2017, I went to see Peter Alliss in The Playhouse at Weston-Super-Mare when he presented a show called 'A Question of Golf', which was billed as an evening of golf anecdotes. At the end of his talk, he threw the session open to questions from the audience and I was first to catch his eye, so I thanked him for his lovely message to my grandson all those years ago. He lied and said, "Yes, I remember it well!" Then he turned to the audience and said, "He still hasn't paid me for it yet!" Brought the house down with laughter – he was such a star. I had taken a copy of my booklet about my marshalling experiences and handed it to the front of house manager with a polite request for Peter to autograph his photograph. During the interval, Peter duly obliged. The last page said, "To be continued…" and Peter wrote, "You bet!" and signed that as well – dated 4th March 2017. When I returned home, I wrote to Peter and thanked him for his kindness. Since his passing away in 2020, there has been no other to take his place as 'The Voice of Golf'.

I'll never forget his comments when trying to work out a player's score and he mentioned the mathematical brilliance of Carol Vorderman on Countdown which he had once watched. He whispered that he got 'AROUSED' – seven letters and not bad for someone who left school at the age of fourteen! You could hear Ken Brown chuckling in the background.

It was a wonderful moment and a testament to Peter's wit and understanding of just how far he could go with his commentary although he was generally thought to have overstepped the mark when, as Zach Johnson collected the Claret Jug in 2015, Peter said that Zach's wife was probably planning a new kitchen! It was a harmless remark but considered by a few to be inappropriate.

Peter Alliss

4th March 2017

THE NEXT CHAPTER

To Be Continued........

You Bet!

MC Alliss
4.3.17

Peter Alliss kindly signed under his photograph in my book and added a quip 'You bet' at the end!

CHAPTER 13 (2016)
THE OPEN (TROON)

My acceptance letter from the R&A didn't arrive until mid-June, which left little time for arranging accommodation. The letter also mentioned a 'uniform fitting session' which I read with some trepidation as I usually found that the shirts and jackets provided were undersized for a man of my bulk. To add to my apprehension, Ralph Lauren would be providing the uniforms. Never having been a dedicated follower of fashion, this paragraph caused a few tremors through my body. The allocation of games was also attached, and I was pleased to see that I had an early one on the final day, which would allow me to get on the road before the main traffic jams.

My accommodation at this event was borne out of sheer luck when I bumped into Keith Woodford at Tebay Services one day as I was heading to Edinburgh. When I told Keith about being unsuccessful in my search, he mentioned a friend of his mother-in-law, who had a room available for rent. She was a single woman whose house had a small annexe with an ensuite bathroom. It was perfect and, although she had a dog, it kept out of the way. Being in a separate part of her house was perfect as I was able to slip out in the early hours of the morning as is my wont. An added benefit was that the house was only eighteen miles from Royal Troon and the journey took less than half an hour at that time in the morning. I always love the excitement of driving to The Open Championship and seeing all the yellow AA directional signs; the surrounding area is so well organised in terms of traffic management.

Keith arriving for breakfast at Tebay Services on M6

It didn't take long to get into the spirit of The Open as the town of Ayr was very busy with visitors when I met up with a few of my fellow scorers one evening and we found ourselves sitting at a table right next to Robert Rock – one of the longest hitters of the golf ball on the European Tour. As we sat down, it was clear that we recognised him and he realised that but, as he was with his partner, we decided to leave him alone and his smile seemed to acknowledge that fact.

On one of the practice days, I bumped into the late John Paramor – the legendary referee – and asked him if I could take a photograph of him. He agreed but, like Ivor Robson, couldn't really understand why anybody would want HIS photograph! John muttered, "Crikey, you are actually taking a photo of me signing my photo! Whatever next?" Like most big men I know, myself included, he was just a nice cuddly person who wouldn't say "Boo" to a goose!

Sadly, John passed away on 20th February 2023. A real loss to the world of golf.

John Paramor and Andy McFee    **John signing his photo**

John's autograph

Humble and courteous, he was known in the golfing world as just 'Big John'. He would be viewed with some trepidation when players spotted him in his buggy watching them. John's attention was generally focussed on ensuring that players kept up with play to ensure that slow play (a feature that Peter Alliss repeatedly decried in his commentary) didn't creep into the game. If a player was 'on the clock', the sight of Big John sitting in his buggy on the top of a nearby mound was enough to spur them along.

I had his photograph printed and with me when I met him at Portrush in 2019 and he was happy to sign it, particularly as he was with Andy McFee, another respected rules official. Making quite an exaggerated flourish when he was signing the photo, he said something along the lines of, "Yet another autograph!" I was probably the first to ask.

The first briefing meeting was followed by a 'uniform fitting' session and, when I turned up there, I said that I would just wear a jacket that I'd purchased from the pro shop with the club logo. That was the routine I had adopted over the years when I found that the ever-diminishing uniform sized didn't fit me. "Oh no you don't!" I was told by the young woman in charge of the fitting area. Ralph Lauren had sponsored the event and part of the deal was the supply of complimentary outfits for the Referees and Scoring Marshals, who were expected to add to the professionalism of the fashion house image out on the golf course.

I felt an air of panic as my waistline had expanded somewhat over the year since I'd last worked at The Open! I was handed my pack and entered the changing room where I tried on the shirt and trousers, neither of which fitted at all. I was called out into the open space outside the cubicle – one of the most embarrassing moments of my life – only for the seamstress, with a safety pin held between her lips, to utter a few words of comfort that it was not a problem. With that, she set about measuring my vital parts and writing notes on the slip of paper which she pinned to the outfit. I was handed a note advising me to return the following day for another fitting.

When I turned up the following day, I was greeted with a wide smile and the seamstress – a young Polish girl – ushered me towards a vacant cubicle where, heart in mouth,

I was to try on my 'amended' outfit. When I opened the plastic bags, I was amazed to see what had been done. The seamstresses had sewn side panels into the shirt thereby increasing the girth by several inches and it fitted just fine. There were two shirts supplied and the second one fitted beautifully as well. They must have used material from another shirt to make the additional panels and I felt guilty at causing additional work for them. I dreaded trying on the trousers as they were of a hipster style and my bum wasn't made for such fashion items. However, not only had they introduced side panels in the legs of the trousers, but they had also increased the depth of the waistband. A truly remarkable feat of engineering and one for which I was eternally grateful. I was able to step out on the course in an outfit that nobody would notice had been extended so meticulously. It was with great relief that I thanked them for their efforts.

On one of the practice days, when I had the opportunity to familiarise myself with the latest developments in the handheld device, I decided to walk with an all-American group – Bubba Watson, Justin Thomas, and J.B. Holmes. I had watched all three at some point on the television at home and it was fascinating to see them have such a fun time together on the course where they were very relaxed and engaging with the spectators.

Bubba about to putt   **Bubba teeing off**

Bubba signing autographs   **Bubba and Doug**

Bubba – twice winner of The Masters (in 2012 and 2014) – was very funny, quipping all the time and making fun of the other two. After analysing their drives, he would step up to the ball and, with minimal messing about, whack it enormous distances. His average driving distance was over 300 yards, and he could hit the ball over 350 yards! His left-handed swing was apparently self-taught and quite unusual, but it worked well.

It was one of the most entertaining mornings in my volunteering career and, after they had finished at the 18th Hole, we had photographs taken together. I wished them well in the Championship. J.B. Holmes did the best out of the threesome, coming third behind Henrik Stenson and Phil Mickelson after that phenomenal battle "down the stretch" as they say on TV.

On Day 2, I walked with the last match out – a South African called Haydn Porteous and two American players whose names escape me. Conditions were awful and we all got soaking wet, but Haydn stood on the last tee and would make the cut if he scored no more than a six. Not a problem, we all thought but how wrong could we be?

In the fading light, and in front of a small group of hardy spectators, Haydn hit his drive over a television compound and out of bounds! We were willing him to make the cut and make sense of why we were still out on the course at about 7:30pm. in the pouring rain. He took dead aim with his third shot – three off the tee – and a par would still allow him to qualify for the weekend. There was almost a collective silent sigh as he carved his drive out to the right and into the television compound, which I thought was out of bounds. However, the Match Referee declared that he could take a free drop from the compound, which meant that he still had an outside chance of making his par with his second ball.

With renewed hope, Haydn hit his next shot to the front edge of the green. Two more shots and he'd be playing the next day. He chipped stone dead and sank the putt by which time visibility was quite poor. We all scuttled off to the R&A hut to register the scores and the two Americans beat a hasty retreat as that was the end of their involvement. However, it was all worthwhile as one of our men had made the cut and somehow soaking wet clothes seemed to be of no consequence! Our team of scoreboard carrier, bunker raker and me were pleased to have seen his achievement. Haydn Porteous and Tom Ridley, his caddie, had to be back out for the first tee off time at 8:30am the following day.

The very next morning, I arrived at the course early as normal and was having a coffee when I spotted Tom Ridley walking briskly towards the coffee stand. I raced over and offered to buy him a drink which he readily accepted, and we stood chatting while he sipped his coffee. He told me that he didn't get to bed until after midnight as he had to dry out all the golf clubs, bag, towels, etc. so it had all been a bit of a rush to get to the course in the morning. It really hit me then how hard the caddies work at times, and I wished him good luck for the remainder of the tournament. I was delighted to observe that his man did progress up the leader board and wasn't in the first group out on the Sunday. In fact, he finished tied 60th.

**Tom Ridley –
Haydn's caddie**

**Matt Corker –
official starter**

Doug with Alex, a scoreboard carrier

One of my undying memories of this event was walking with Dustin Johnson and watching his extraordinary hitting of the golf ball. He could hit a golf ball even further than Bubba Watson. On one occasion he was the only player to drive a Par 4 hole and I'll never forget the sound of his ball travelling through the air – like a bullet! Dustin always had a very relaxed look about him with that swagger than made him look like a gunslinger from the western movies.

When I visited The Open Shop, I noticed that they were engraving ball markers and, as a special gift to my friends back home, I had a few engraved with their names on the rear of a rather large marker with the Claret Jug logo on the front. Contained in a black pouch, they were a great present to hand out on my return home.

Since Ivor Robson retired in 2015, the announcing arrangements changed at Troon with the appointment of two gentlemen who were to share the duties on the first tee. David Lancaster and Matt Corker took it in turns to announce the players and that is where I first met Matt Corker.

It was my habit to make my way to the first tee well before play started at 6:30am to bag a seat at the front of the stand behind the tee. It was by far the best place to soak up the atmosphere of The Open and see first-hand so many golfing greats as they walked out on to the tee. I would generally bump into Kim, a lovely lady from the Atlanta in the USA, and we would sit and chat until the first players arrived on the tee. I first met Kim at Hoylake in 2006. I recall one conversation where we observed that the American players generally wore well-tailored trousers (pants) whereas the European players tended to wear tight jeans-like trousers, which didn't look quite so smart. We found many topics to discuss as we waited for the next group of players to arrive on the tee.

It was there that I first introduced Matt to Kim (from Atlanta). We were waiting for play to start on Day 1 of The Open. Thereafter, Matt always made a point of saying "hello" to Kim and me on the first tee – a very special welcome at such a prestigious event! It was a great feeling of continuity because gentleman Ivor Robson always made a point of saying 'Good morning' to us when he spotted us sitting close by in the stand.

Kim and Beth from Atlanta

Doug posing on 1st Tee

Justin Thomas and Doug

I have become a very close friend of Matt Corker, who works closely with David Lancaster. In fact, when Matt was on rest periods, he usually came and sat with me in the stand around the first tee. Once or twice, he had brought me some 'goodies' from the first tee in the form of Mars Bars or KitKats – ever the gentleman.

In the final day's play at Royal Troon in 2016, I walked with Paul Lawrie and Danny Willett who had just won The Masters earlier that year. Strangely enough, I was going to withdraw that morning as my knee was hurting but, when I walked into Scoring HQ, the Chief Scorer said that tee times had been brought forward but my match time would remain, which meant I wasn't walking with the pairing that had been posted on the day's play. I can't remember who I was down to walk with – two American players that I didn't know – but I was going to be happy to let the reserve scorer take my place. However, the revised timetable meant that I would be accompanying Paul Lawrie and Danny Willett! My knee suddenly felt a whole lot better and when was I going to get another opportunity to score for Paul Lawrie – one of my favourite players and past winner of The Open Championship together with the current Masters Champion?

What a result.

On the 7th hole, most players were having a go at driving the green on this 400-plus yards hole. Danny Willett's drive ended up approximately 50 yards short of the green and, after a lengthy conversation with his caddie, he chipped his ball short of the green! He turned to his caddie and issued the longest string of expletives that I have ever heard on any golf course, and I must confess that I cringed at the thought of youngsters in the crowd catching what he was shouting.

After they had played the next hole – the famous Postage Stamp – we headed off up the ninth fairway and Danny nipped into a portaloo to relieve himself. I strolled alongside his caddie and asked him how he coped with such an unprovoked assault on his eardrums like I had just witnessed. His response was along the lines of that "it was better for Danny to vent at him than keep his emotions bottled up inside". I guess that is good anger management but, in my humble opinion, Danny needs to be careful about who is listening nearby. Had it been picked up by one of the many television microphones around the course, some commentator would be apologising to the viewers for the bad language!

Later in the day, after I had walked with Match No.10, I was heading back towards the course when I met Henrik Stenson walking through the car park. I approached him and shook his hand, wishing him good luck in the afternoon. As usual, he was gracious and thanked me for my good wishes. Later, I tried to convince myself that my handshake had imparted to him the good fortune that he needed to go and win the championship, which indeed he had! Always the perfect gentleman and I have long been a fan of the way he relates to youngsters, and the way that he readily gives them his time. He is a solid guy.

The battle between Phil Mickelson and Henrik Stenson was labelled by Tom Watson as being the best golf he had seen at a championship, eclipsing his own battle with Jack Nicklaus in 1977, entitled 'The Duel in The Sun', which they played out at Turnberry. Press reports described the final day's golf at Troon as being like two heavyweight prize fighters slugging out a boxing match. Henrik Stenson – 'The Iceman' – prevailed and won by three shots from the gallant Mickelson who gave it his all.

They received a standing ovation as they walked down the 18th fairway. After the event, Henrik reported that he had received a hand-written letter from Jack Nicklaus saying that it was the best golf he had ever seen.

Autographed flag to be auctioned for charity

Jordan Spieth signing flag

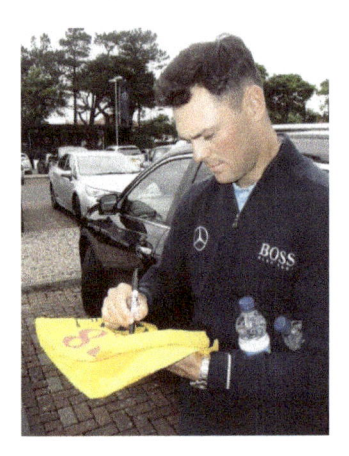

and Martin Kaymer

A friend of mine – Stewart Galway, Captain of Tickenham Golf club at the time - asked me to get players to sign a flag so that the item could then be auctioned off to raise money for charity. Players were happy to do so, and I managed to get quite a few autographs from some of the top players who were at The Open Championship.

CHAPTER 14 (2018)
THE OPEN (CARNOUSTIE)

When my acceptance letter arrived in the post in early March, my thoughts immediately turned to finding suitable accommodation. The letter also mentioned that uniforms would now be supplied by Hugo Boss – that was my second introduction to fashion in the space of two years. The allocation was to include two polo shirts, one jacket, one pair of trousers, a belt (thank goodness for that) and one cap.

Finding accommodation, as I have said before, was always a dilemma; whether to book somewhere in the hope of being selected or wait until selection then hunt around for something suitable. I usually tapped into my network of marshals but, of course, they were usually on the hunt as well.

Arranging accommodation for this tournament was quite a challenge with most local hotels and B&Bs hiking their prices for that period. The only available room I could find was in a B&B which wanted to charge me £3,500.00 for ten nights, yes £3,500.00. I almost swallowed my false teeth! The truth of the situation was that, if I wasn't prepared to pay that exorbitant charge, someone else would. The Open Championship attracts lots of Americans to the UK and they usually are prepared to pay the inflated costs as part of their overall costs for the trip. I couldn't afford that kind of money and felt rather depressed that, having been given the job that I wanted, I might have to withdraw.

In a chance conversation with my oldest brother, David (whom I should explain had spent considerable time in Carnoustie researching our family history as my father was born there), he enquired what establishment could be charging such excessive rates and I gave him the name of the B&B. David pointed out that the building had been built by our paternal great-grandfather, Alexander Fowler, whose name was on the foundation stone of the building! David had noticed that on one of his trips to Carnoustie while doing his research. What a coincidence!

Armed with that information, I decided to try and negotiate a more reasonable rate by mentioning my family connection. The owner thought about this new information and, after some consideration, said the immortal words, "In that case, you can have the room for the knock-down price of only three thousand pounds."

Such a concession I could do without, and I decided to look around for alternative accommodation.

I managed to contact an old school friend, Bruce, who lived in nearby Letham, some twelve miles or so north of Carnoustie. I had only recently renewed our acquaintance after fifty years when we went our separate ways after leaving school. In fact, the accommodation I was offered was ideal as my school pal had a ground-floor room with ensuite facilities, so I could come and go without disturbing the family when I left at some early hour. The perfect arrangement. My stars had aligned once more.

Serendipity again, as I was able to renew a friendship with someone I hadn't seen since 1967. We had always gotten on well at school but, like so many relationships at that young age, we moved on and away from our alma mater.

After my visit to the course each day, I would return to Letham and be served with a lovely dinner followed by a wee dram while we reminisced about our schoolboy days in Buckie. Bruce wouldn't charge me for staying at his place, but I was able to take him and his wife, Jeannie, out to her favourite restaurant in nearby Forfar for dinner on my last night with them. In addition, I was able to make a substantial contribution to their local church charity, and still had plenty of change from £3,000.00! It really was a win-win situation all round.

Rabbits with beers   **Smartly dressed gentlemen**

Sometimes spectators will wear outfits that ensure the television cameras will focus on them at some point although I doubt whether wearing a rabbit costume would get them recognised on screen! The odd thing is that I asked them to smile while I took the photograph.

As at most of The Open Championships I attended, entry was through a marquee which had been set up with security scanners and spectators would be asked to open their bags and have a quick 'frisk' to ensure that they had no offensive weapons or the like. Over the entrance, was a huge sign, saying: 'Welcome to The Open'. On the other side, was the opposite saying: 'Have a safe journey home', together with a smaller sign saying: 'This way to the Train Station', which always made me cringe. I could hear my friend's voice in my head saying, *It's a Railway Station!* Although I was well known for being an English language pedant myself, I'd never quite got that one right with my friend, Jane.

The nostalgia of visiting my father's hometown was very strong as brother, David, had sent me a book about the town together with a map. As the house I was brought up in was called Carlogie, I was fascinated to see streets like Carlogie Street and so on.

During one of the practice days, when we were allowed out on the course to familiarise ourselves with the updated handheld computer devices, Ronnie Nichol and I asked Bernhard Langer if he would mind having our company as he set off to play a few holes on his own. Gracious as ever, Bernhard agreed and simply asked that we kept off to his left and out of his eyeline, something that we were trained to do anyway. Having walked with him at The Belfry in 2002, I was delighted to see that he was still competing at the highest level, a mark of the man's resilience and determination.

We were both taken with Bernhard's meticulous approach to his practice, sometimes hitting as many as five or six balls from the same position. He would walk around a green, hitting shots from the rough, the bunkers (much to the feigned delight of his caddy) and followed that routine by several hitting putts from various part of the green where the caddy had placed tee pegs showing the pin positions for the first two days. It was quite clear to see why Bernhard was able to compete at the highest level in events such as The Open Championship even though he had progressed to the Seniors' Tour.

Bernhard had never won The Open Championship, but he was a past winner at The Masters back in 1993. He had won The Senior Open Championship in 2013 and clearly had what it takes, looking the model of fitness at the ripe old age of 61. I'll never forget his captaincy of the European Team at the Ryder Cup in 2004 when he displayed all the hallmarks of a great leader and planner. Ronnie and I were grateful for his patience and thanked him for allowing us the privilege of walking with him. We left him to it after about six holes. A great man, a great player and fabulous to spend time with him.

Signed photograph of Bernhard Langer

While walking on course with the top golfing professionals, there are lots of opportunities to chat to their caddies who generally are quite happy to engage with Walking Scorers – and it probably reduces the likelihood that we are going to disturb the players. At Carnoustie, I was walking with Webb Simpson of the USA and started to chat to his caddie while Webb nipped into an on-course portaloo. We chatted for what seemed like an eternity and the Match Referee walked over and asked if Webb was OK – he had been in there for over five minutes! His caddie explained that Webb had overindulged the night before and had eaten a strong curry! Enough said. Webb emerged from the portaloo looking pale and wan, but he still managed an eagle at the following Par 5 hole!

As usual at these events, I would get up early and head for the course to maximise the opportunities for photographs and autographs. On the Monday of The Open, I wandered into Gather – a lovely deli – and I decided to have breakfast. There were only two other people in there and I didn't pay much attention to them as I headed for a high stool near a shelf in the window; that way I could keep a sharp lookout for players in the street outside. As I was waiting, I could hear the two other guests chatting, one in a Deep South drawl – clearly from the USA.

For once in my life, I decided not to engage other people in conversation, so I left the Americans to enjoy their breakfast in peace. As they walked out the door, past my position in the window, I could see that it was Dustin Johnson (World No.1) and his caddie! How I rued the fact that I had missed such an opportunity. The girls behind the counter came over and asked me if that man was someone famous. I told them that he was the World No.1! They freaked out and immediately got on their mobile phones to boyfriends or partners.

I went into the same deli the following morning and Dustin Johnson was there again. I couldn't resist saying, "Good morning, Dustin. Good luck in the tournament." He smiled and said, "Thank you." The girls were giving him extra special attention – with their knowledge of who he was – so I decided not to approach him with a request for a photograph or autograph. That was hard for me! People who know me will understand how difficult it was for me not to engage Dustin in conversation at first meeting as the opportunity was there to be taken. Nevertheless, I fought off my basic instinct and decided that, as Dustin was using a local establishment, it was best to respect his privacy and leave him alone.

However, on the third day (Wednesday), I could contain myself anymore and walked over to Dustin's table with the offer to buy him breakfast (I knew I had to do something extraordinary so as not to appear like a sycophantic fan!).

Dustin was visibly moved by my offer (he is worth millions, and I am not) and gratefully accepted. In fact, it was probably quite a surprise to him that a Scot should show such generosity, given the myth that Scottish people are mean spirited. I don't know where that impression came from because all the Scots that I know are really generous to a fault.

On my way out, I casually said goodbye to him and headed over to the cash till to stump up. As Linda was preparing my receipt – I asked for a pristine copy – Dustin came over and asked me if I wanted a photograph. I quipped, "I don't do photographs," which made him laugh. However, I had a couple of photographs taken with him (he is tall) and left with my chest bursting with pride! Of course, I have dined out on that story many times since!

Staff at Gather – a superb deli in Carnoustie

Dustin Johnson and Doug

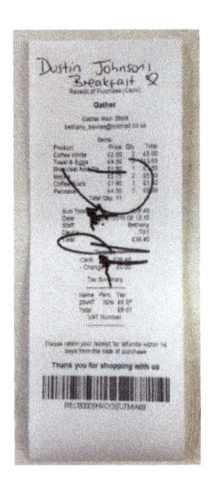

Dustin's bill

At The Open, one of my favourite places was the Open Arms; a great name which belied the usual rip-off prices that were charged within. Behind a long bar, there would be an equally long trestle table behind which there was an array of beer pumps which were on the go almost continuously. When you bought a round of drinks, the bartender would take your cash and hand you a cardboard beer carrier with four almost-filled pints of beer – lager in the main. Spectators would generally move quickly outside with their drinks unless it was raining, in which case the place became a crush of queues and groups standing about. The organisers cunningly failed to provide tables for obvious reasons and any standing tables would be crammed with plastic beer glasses.

The fish & chips place was usually next door, and a queuing system would ensure that 'first come first served' worked. The choice was fish and chips or… fish and chips! By the entrance/exit there would be a table with sauces and condiments which ended up in a right mess as most customers had been to the beer tent first. At the front of the food counter, was a tray with chocolate bars, KitKats and the like. I never could resist buying a couple and putting them in my bag for later. 'Later' was usually five minutes after I had finished the fish and chips.

I would normally take my food and drink to one of the picnic-style benches and sit wherever there was a space. I had interesting conversations with lots of spectators, who were always intrigued by my Scorer's lanyard and security pass badge. They generally wanted to know what exactly I did, and I always took the trouble to explain our role in detail. It was not unusual to be talking to someone from Canada one minute then Ireland the next and so on. The truly international feel of The Open Championship always fascinated me as it showed how a common interest in sport – any sport – would unite complete strangers, some of whom I am still in contact with to this day. Sitting on these benches was also a great spot for people-watching – one of my favourite activities at such events – and it was remarkable how often I would see an old friend or a celebrity just mingling in the crowd. Mind you, some of the strange outfits that were worn by spectators ensured that the television cameras would swing round to them and result in a funny comment from the likes of Peter Alliss. I have photographs of a bunch of white rabbits, which I have already mentioned, but never quite worked out the connection with golf!

Canadian supporters at The Open   **USA fan**

Doug with spectators

After completing my stint at Carnoustie, I received a lovely letter of thanks from Chris Healey, the Chief Scorer, in which she said, "We all appreciate the effort and commitment that you have put in, especially on Friday when the weather conditions can only be described as challenging." Understatement of the year. I also received a lovely letter from the Dunnichen Letham and Kirkden Church for my donation to their church funds, for which they said they were very grateful "especially as you live so far away".

Shortly after working at The Open Championship that year, I had the pleasure of playing golf in the Lions Club of Budleigh Salterton Charity Golf Day played over the gorgeous course at East Devon Golf Club. I played in a team comprising my son Chris, his son Ben, my son-in-law Paul and me. I had lived in Budleigh Salterton between 1977 and 1985 when I had been a founder member of the Lions Club with the honour of being its first President. I had remained in touch with my friends in the Lions Club and had attended each of their golf days since they were first launched. I love the photograph of Ben teeing off as it shows the town of Budleigh Salterton with a section of the beautiful coastline east towards Sidmouth and beyond. I have a canvas print of that photograph on my wall at home – not only the lovely view but a perfect backswing too!

Chris, Paul, Ben and Doug

Ben teeing off on the 16th Hole at East Devon Golf Club

CHAPTER 15 (2019)
THE OPEN (ROYAL PORTRUSH)

One of my most treasured letters of acceptance was the one I received from Angela Wilson, Chief Scorer at Royal Portrush, as I was so excited at the thought of returning to Ireland for only the second time in my life. My first visit, of course, was to the Ryder Cup Matches in 2006.

Having enjoyed such success with my accommodation at Hoylake in 2006, I tried the same approach when looking for accommodation in Portrush in 2019. I scoured the Internet for churches in and around Portrush and this was one of the first replies that I received:

"Good morning, Doug,

I sent your email on to Rev John and we both had a chat about it today. We do have an apartment in our church that we sometimes rent out to ministers or other people involved in a mission of whatever kind and at the moment we have no one in it over the golf. It is a 2-bedroom, 2-bathroom apartment with a lounge area (all this is upstairs) and our offices are also upstairs. We converted the Old Manse on Main Street in Portrush just beside our church. The kitchen is downstairs (cooker, microwave, kettle etc but no washing machine) and would be shared with whatever group if any and by us the workers during the day, but that shouldn't bother you. We would rent the main ensuite double room out to you and you would have your own key and could come and go whenever it suits you. If this would be acceptable to you the rate is £50 per day. We are approx. 6 minutes' walk to the golf course, and I can actually see it from my window as I work. I have the best view from any office window (you must come and see while you are here).

We would be very happy to have you and can assure you that our little apartment is very cosy. As it is on Main Street and the Open is on, obviously the town will be quite busy at night-time, but you have been to other golf events, so you know the idea. Portrush is lovely when the sun shines and I really hope the weather will be favourable for you while you are here. There is a launderette on the road you will walk down to the golf if you need it.

Please let me know what you think and if this would be suitable for you."

When that email message popped up, I just sat and stared at my computer screen, not believing in my luck. Perhaps I should resume my church attendance that I had forsaken back in the late 1960s!

I couldn't believe my eyes, and I couldn't wait to call my mate, Ronnie, who had entrusted me to find accommodation for us, but he had rejected a couple of B&B offers which in his words "were just too big". In other words, too expensive.

Having seen overnight rates of over £100.00, it was almost inconceivable that I was being offered a rate of just £50.00 per night. First, I had to check that it was OK for me to bring a friend, but the church administrator readily agreed that it would be fine.

When I rang Ronnie to impart the great news, his first reaction was that I was winding him up but, as the reality dawned, he got excited about the reality of a place right in the middle of the town.

"Near so many pubs!" was his main reaction.

Not only had I secured us accommodation, but I had a place where the car would be parked safely – behind the manse in a gated area. Ronnie suggested that, as I would be in Portrush from the Thursday before the golf started, that I may like to collect him from the ferry port in Belfast thereby meaning that he wouldn't have to take his car, he could travel as foot passenger – his ferry was leaving from Scotland (he lives in Ayr) whereas I would be taking the ferry from Birkenhead.

This worked out as it meant that I had a few days to sightsee before Ronnie joined me and I was able to savour the delights of the Giant's Causeway and the like. The filming of *Game of Thrones* also took place along that coastline, so it was like a holiday within a holiday, and I vowed that I would return for a proper look around at some point in the future.

At that time, little did I know that The Open Championship was such a success in Northern Ireland that the R&A squeezed in a return visit to Royal Portrush in 2025 (and, yes, I have already secured the same apartment although at a somewhat more expensive rate – at the time of writing this, Ronnie has not yet confirmed that he is going to attend but that is immaterial to me as I'm sure I'll find another marshal happy to bunk in with me! When I called to check that the apartment would be available, I was told that someone was already making enquiries about its availability for The Open, but I would be given first refusal. What clinched the deal was that I promised to do a pen and ink drawing of the building as a present for their generosity and cooperation!).

As soon as the accommodation was confirmed and my job as a scorer was ratified, I sent an email to Matt Corker – the official starter at The Open (well, one of two along with David Lancaster, his boss!) – advising him that I hadn't retired from scoring after all as the Irish gig was too good to turn down, especially in view of the accommodation already being sorted. His reply was simply:

"Excellent news.

I'll be the handsome one on the 1st tee...look out for me!!"

MC

A man of few words.

First Tee at Royal Portrush

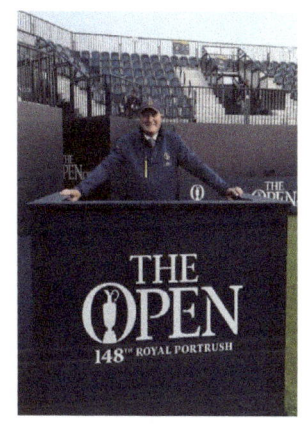

David Lancaster – Official Starter

Matt and David posing with spectators

Doug with Angela - Chief Scorer

Ronnie arrived in Belfast on the Sunday before The Open as we had to attend a training session on the Monday. I took a trip along the County Antrim coastline on my way south to Belfast, calling in at every small harbour along the way. The scenery was evocative of my homeland in Banffshire, and I realised how fishing communities evolved in similar ways because they faced similar challenges. Ronnie looked a bedraggled figure as I collected him from the ferry port. He had just completed three days of scoring at The Scottish Open and had foregone the final day's play there to make the journey over from Scotland via Cairnryan Ferry Port. (It was known as Stranraer for 150 years, but the ferries moved out in 2011 to allow Stranraer to expand as a maritime centre).

We had a blast in Portrush, spilling out into the night air after a day's work at the golf. I recall the crowd outside the Portrush Harbour Bar and posing for photographs with a couple of lovely local ladies. Ronnie's attention was soon diverted, and he suddenly disappeared only to return with a big grin on his face.

"I've just been chatting to Rich Beem, the golfing guy off the telly!"

Truth be told, Rich was a former Major winner having beaten off none other than Tiger Woods to unexpectedly win the PGA Championship in 2002. He was in Portrush working for Sky TV.

That was one of the fascinating things about the game of golf as, unlike football players, the top golfers could mingle with the crowds in a very informal way. As if to emphasise that point, the reason that we had difficulty getting into the pub in the first place was that Darren Clarke was in there drinking with the locals. On my way to the golf course the following day, I passed Dame Laura Davies and greeted her with a casual, "Good morning, Dame Laura." She appeared to appreciate the informality and the fact that I didn't take the chance encounter as an opportunity to ask for a 'selfie'. Little did she know how much my inner voice had to stop me doing so, saying, *Leave the poor woman alone, she's obviously in a hurry!*

During an Open Championship, another activity that I enjoyed was to wander round the merchandising shop to buy ball markers for my friends back home; they always appreciated a shiny ball marker with the distinctive Open logo (the Claret Jug). These weren't cheap by any means but were lovely gifts for any golfer.

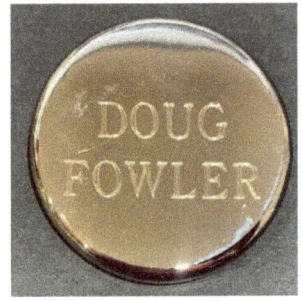

Engraved ball marker

As with previous experiences at The Open, I realised that my uniform fitting exercise would be a challenge for the seamstress team, and I brought along my jacket, shirt, and trousers from the last event so that they could use them as templates for the adjustments they had to make. The same Polish woman oversaw fitting, and she greeted me with a wide smile, saying, "Here we go again – another challenge!" Although the shirt fitted snugly, I didn't ever remove my jacket as I didn't think that the paying public deserved such a sight while enjoying their golf. How I wished that I had lost some weight to make her job easier. If anything, their expertise in sorting out the fitting problem probably resulted in my making less of an effort in that regard. Again, she did a wonderful job of fitting me with a super outfit.

I have a box of shirts and jackets that have been handed to me at the beginning of tournaments, none of which fit as it seems the Far East manufacturers' idea of XXXL is equivalent to a Medium in the United Kingdom. Perhaps I will have an auction one day and make a few pounds for charity.

I was just leaving the recorder's hut one day, when I spotted Danny Willett waiting to be interviewed after his round and I asked him if I could take his photograph. He agreed and asked me to wait a couple of moments while he sorted out something in his golf bag. While I was standing waiting patiently, Jordan Spieth grabbed my mobile and took a 'selfie' with me!

"That's the way to do it!" - he said as he handed back my mobile 'phone.

Jordan Spieth and Doug 'selfie'

Doug and Danny Willett – photo by Jordan Spieth

As I said before, I usually like to take home some golfing memorabilia from The Open Championship and, having bought a bright red cap, I was going to try and get it signed by Rory McIlroy. This was easier said than done because security around the players was tight and it wasn't easy to get to him for any chance of an autograph. However, I learned that one of the administrators in the Scorers' HQ was married to the Captain of Royal Portrush Golf Club – Robert Barry - so I thought it would be possible for him, through his connections, to get my cap signed by Rory. To be fair, he did take it into the pro shop for Rory to sign but, as we all know, Rory didn't make the cut and he disappeared on the Friday evening.

Robert Barry – Royal Portrush Captain

Alice – a Walking Scorer – told me that she lived in one of the houses nearby

After all, this was The Open being played at his home course where he held the record for the lowest round and his failure to make the cut obviously hurt him deeply. After a disastrous opening round 79 that included a quadruple-bogey 8 on the first hole, a triple-bogey 7 on the last and a missed putt from a foot on the par-3 16th, it would have taken some heavy lifting up the leader board for the 30-year-old four-time major champion just to make it to the weekend.

And on Friday, he nearly did it. He carded a 65 but it that was one shot too many!

I should add here that, when I boast about some top golfer that I have met, my brother – Alex – usually tops it by casually saying, "I find Princess Anne is the easiest of The Royal Family to talk to!" Of course, it does me no good to correct him by adding that a preposition is a bad thing to end a sentence with! He has been to several garden parties in both Holyrood Palace and Buckingham Palace in his role as President of the RNLI in Scotland.

On the last day, I wasn't down to work, but the Chief Scorer asked if I would go out with the first game, which was a 'singleton', Ashton Turner (Eng), who was down to play with the local club professional Gary McNeill at 7:32am. On the first tee, Gary received a louder cheer than Ashton, much to the amusement of everyone around the tee AND Gary outdrove him.

At the end of the round, before walking by the 18th Green, I stopped for a moment and took out my mobile phone to capture the scene one last time. The Match Referee – a tall Norwegian whose name I forget – walked over to me and I thought I was about to be reprimanded for using my phone on the course, and me an official! He whispered to me that he didn't realise it was OK to take photos and he promptly took out his mobile and started snapping away himself.

Shortly afterwards, I was chatting to Gary outside the clubhouse, and I asked if I could have a photograph taken with him. He readily agreed so I handed my camera to the nearest person who happened to be none other than Pat Jennings OBE! I told him that I had met him in 2006 at The K Club but he really couldn't remember – why should he?!

Club professional Gary McNeill and Doug

Doug with Pat Jennings OBE (again)

Having completed our respective rounds, Ronnie and I went to the Tented Village to watch the conclusion of the championship with Shane Lowry eventually winning, having led from the front for much of the week. Such a fitting result for an event that hadn't been held in Ireland since 1951. We settled down to watch the action on the big screen along with a few thousand other spectators. Unfortunately, the heavens opened, and we had to scuttle into The Open Arms (aptly named) along with everyone else. This crush somehow heightened the camaraderie, and the atmosphere was unforgettable as Shane finally received the Claret Jug.

The crowd of spectators watching the big screen in the tented village as Shane Lowry wins The Open

Rhoda, Doug and Alex

in Scorers' HQ

At 237,000 spectators, all previous Open Championship records were broken.

I frequently watch *University Challenge* on television, and I have a personal challenge with a very good friend of mine when we compare notes after the end of the programme and commiserate with each other. However, I recall one evening when the starter question showed a map of the United Kingdom with a star on Sandwich, Kent. The question was, "The Open Golf Championship is played at courses around the UK – can you name this location?"

Of course, I jumped to attention and shouted, "Sandwich!" which none of the contestants got right.

For once, I felt like the clever ones on the programme when the bonus questions were posed after the next starter was answered correctly. Three other locations were located with a star: Carnoustie, Hoylake and Portrush, all of which I knew having been to each one as a volunteer. I could have been clever and said, "Royal St George's, Carnoustie, Royal Liverpool and Royal Portrush," but I didn't. For once in my life, I felt like those students must feel when answering questions correctly and they know the answer in great detail. It also dawned on me that I would have to live to be about three hundred to gain the knowledge that they regularly display.

CHAPTER 16 (2022) THE FUTURE – THE OPEN 2025 (ROYAL PORTRUSH)

Since my involvement at Portrush, I haven't carried out any scoring duties mainly due to the pandemic and a horrendous accident that I suffered on a building site in June 2021. Due to the negligence of a builder, the site wasn't safe, and I unwittingly fell into an unprotected hole (which had been cut out for the installation of a shower waste) while taking dimensions in a first-floor room.

The flooring was covered with black plastic due to high-level windows not yet being installed. Therefore, the unprotected hole was hidden from view and, not realising this, I stepped right on the hidden hole and my right leg went right through with the result that I nearly lost the leg (and indeed my life as I was bleeding out when I rang on my mobile for help to come quickly). I was rushed to A&E and patched up before having plastic surgery to cover the deep wound a few days later. My leg still looks like a shark has taken a chunk out of it and I am unable to walk easily without the aid of a walking stick!

I have been limited to accompanying my friends around the golf course in a buggy. I recently went round with them at the Bristol and Clifton Golf Club which my playing partner, Jayne, had joined and she was pleased to show us around the lovely course. I leapt out of the buggy from time to time for a spot of putting which made me yearn to be back on the golf course and that is now my primary aim.

Stewart, Jayne, George, Suzie and Andrew

It was a great disappointment to me that I didn't make it the 150th Open at St Andrews in 2022, despite writing to the R&A asking if they would consider me for a desk-bound job. They were understandably overwhelmed with applications for that event, which I watched with envy on the television. It really was a great celebration of golf and I enjoyed the coverage from the knowledge of being familiar with the course and many of the volunteers participating in making a piece of golfing history.

St Andrews set up for the 150th Open Championship.

Although I didn't make it to St Andrews for the 150th Open Championship, I bought a few commemorative caps and sent them to family and friends as a gift to celebrate the end of my scoring days. Below are photographs of two of my brothers who play golf – Alex and Ian.

Alex **Ian**

Ben – my grandson

Paul – my son-in-law

Jayne, my mixed foursomes partner

Andrew, friend

Vern, my friend from USA

Dave, friend

Doug

In 2025, when The Open returns to Royal Portrush, I am hoping to be fit enough again to carry out duties as a Walking Scorer. It would be the final act in my now comprehensive Golf Marshalling CV which looks like this:

Profile

Highly experienced volunteer marshal/scorer working with the R&A and the European Tour at major golfing championships throughout England, Scotland, Ireland and Wales.

Achievements

- Operated scoreboard at The Open (twice);
- Operated as walking scorer at The Open (8 times) and the Ryder Cup (twice);
- Promoted to Senior Marshal (Scoring) for Wales Open in 2003;
- Pioneered system of introducing scorers to Starter and Players for European Tour in 2004;
- Trialled GPS scoring system at The Wales Open 2005;
- Wrote guidelines for scorers at The Wales Open in 2007

Experience

- Marshal at The English Open 2000/2001/2002 (Forest of Arden);
- Marshal at British Seniors PGA Championship 2000 (The Belfry);
- Marshal at The Wales Open 2001 – 2003 (Celtic Manor);
- Marshal at Great North Open 2002 (Slaley Hall);
- Walking Scorer at The Ryder Cup 2002 (The Belfry);
- Scoreboard Operator at **The Open 2003** (Royal St. George's);
- Senior Marshal (Scoring) at The Wales Open 2003 - 2007 (Celtic Manor);
- Scoring Marshal at The British Masters 2004 - 2008 (Forest of Arden);
- Scoreboard Operator at **The Open 2005** (St. Andrews);
- Walking Scorer at **The Open 2006** (Hoylake);
- Walking Scorer at The Ryder Cup 2006 (The K Club - Dublin);
- Walking Scorer at **The Open 2010** (St. Andrews);
- Walking Scorer at **The Open 2011** (Royal St. George's);
- Walking Scorer at **The Open 2016** (Royal Troon);
- Walking Scorer at **The Open 2018** (Carnoustie);
- Walking Scorer at **The Open 2019** (Portrush).

Interests

I am very keen on being involved at golf tournaments and I have given talks to local golf clubs about my experiences as a scorer at The Ryder Cup Matches as well as The Open.

It's a record of which I am immensely proud, and it charts the many experiences I have had at some of the top golf tournaments in the twenty-year period from my first excursion to The Forest of Arden in 2000.

My negotiations for accommodation in Portrush started as soon as I heard that, due to the success of the 2019 event, the R&A had decided that a return should be inserted into their future schedule and The Open Championship will return to Royal Portrush in 2025. I don't know if I will be fit enough to carry out the duties of Walking Scorer in 2025, but I shall make every effort to ensure that I am as fit as can be. In any case, I had such a good time when I last visited that I would be happy to return as a spectator. Ronnie hasn't yet confirmed that he will be joining me this next time and, if he doesn't, I'm sure I won't have a problem finding someone to join me at that venue.

I look forward to meeting up with old friends and signing copies of this book! That would be a fitting end to my volunteering career which, when it started, I never for a moment imagined that my autograph would be in demand!

I would also like to thank all the officials at the R&A for entrusting me with such responsible roles over the years.

ACKNOWLEDGEMENTS

My first acknowledgement must go to John Wardle for having the confidence in me all those years ago. I thoroughly enjoyed working with him, and his deputy Peter Houghton, without whom I would never have progressed to the larger stage of scoring at The Ryder Cup Matches and The Open Championship. John still sends me a Christmas card, which usually features one of his wonderful watercolour paintings.

Barry and Mavis Drew gave me every opportunity to commit to helping them run an efficient service for the European Tour. Despite our falling out in 2008, I owe them so much for their support over the years that I worked with them. I hear that they have now retired, and they deserve to put their feet up and relax.

I would also like to thank all the officials at the R&A for entrusting me with such responsible roles over the years.

Bob and Moira Cameron of Lundin Links for their hospitality when I worked at St Andrews in 2005 and 2010.

Bruce and Jeannie Mair for their hospitality when I worked at Carnoustie in 2018.

Reverend John and Alison for their accommodation when I worked at Portrush in 2019.

To all the marshals who have helped me along the way and from whom I have learned so much.

To all the players who have tolerated my intrusions into their privacy when asking for photograph opportunities and their caddies too.

APPENDIX – Winners (The Open in blue) and runners up in brackets:

2000 – The Compass Group English Open (Forest of Arden) – Darren Clarke -13 (Michael Campbell, Mark James).

2001 – The Celtic Manor Resort Wales Open – Paul McGinley -6 (Paul Lawrie, Darren Lee) Play off.

2001 – The Compass Group English Open (Forest of Arden) – Peter O'Malley -13 (Raphael Jacquelin).

2002 – The Great North Open (Slaley Hall) Miles Tunnicliff -9 (Sven Struver).

2002 – The Celtic Manor Resort Wales Open – Paul Lawrie -16 (John Bickerton).

2002 - The Compass Group English Open (Forest of Arden) – Darren Clarke -17 (Soren Hansen).

2002 - The Ryder Cup (The Belfry – Brabazon) – Europe 15½ to 12½.

2003 – The Celtic Manor Resort Wales Open – Ian Poulter -18 (Darren Fichardt, Jonathan Lomas, Jarrod Moseley).

2003 – The Open (Sandwich) – Ben Curtis -1 (Thomas Bjorn & Vijay Singh).

2004 – The Celtic Manor Wales Open – Simon Khan -21 (Paul Casey) Play off.

2004 – The Daily Telegraph Damovo British Masters (Forest of Arden) – Barry Lane -16 (Angel Cabrera & Eduardo Romero).

2005 – The Celtic Manor Wales Open – Miguel Angel Jimenez -14 (Martin Erlandsson & Jose Manuel Lara).

2005 – The Open (St Andrews) – Tiger Woods -14 (Colin Montgomerie).

2006 – The Celtic Manor Wales Open – Robert Karlsson -16 (Paul Broadhurst).

2006 - The Open (Hoylake) – Tiger Woods -18 (Chris DiMarco).

2006 – The Ryder Cup (K Club-Palmer North) – Europe – 18½ to 9½.

2007 – The Celtic Manor Wales Open – Richard Sterne -13 (Bradley Dredge, Soren Kjeldsen, Mardan Mamat, Mads Vide-Hastrup).

2008 – The Celtic Manor Wales Open – Scott Strange -22 (Robert Karlsson) – I left on Saturday!

2008 - The Quinn Insurance British Masters (The Belfry) – Gonzalo Fernandez-Castano -12 (Lee Westwood) Play off.

2010 – The Open (St Andrews) – Louis Oosthuizen -16 (Lee Westwood).

2011 – The Open (Sandwich) – Darren Clarke – 5 (Dustin Johnson & Phil Mickelson).

2016 – The Open (Troon) – Henrik Stenson -20 (Phil Mickelson).

2018 – The Open (Carnoustie) – Francesco Molinari – 8 (Kevin Kisner, Rory McIlroy, Justin Rose, Xander Schauffele).

2019 – The Open (Portrush) – Shane Lowry -15 (Tommy Fleetwood).

2022 – The Future – The Open (Portrush in 2025)

Milton Keynes UK
Ingram Content Group UK Ltd.
UKHW020011100923
428402UK00005B/21

9 781803 697468